chet baker

chet baker

his life and music

j. de valk

berkeley hills books

berkeley california

Published by:
Berkeley Hills Books, PO Box 9877, Berkeley, California 94709 USA

Copyright:
© 1989 Van Gennep
This translation and revision copyright © 2000 Berkeley Hills Books

LCCN: 00-104178

Library of Congress Cataloging-in-Publication Data:
Valk, Jeroen de, 1958–
   [Chet Baker. English]
   Chet Baker : his life and music / by Jeroen de Valk.
     p. cm.
   Includes bibliographical references, discography, and index.
   Translation of: Chet Baker : herinneringen aan een lyrisch trompettist.
   ISBN 1-893163-13-X (alk. paper)
   1. Baker, Chet. 2. Jazz musicians—United States—Biography. I. Title.
ML419.B14 V313 2000
788.9'2165'092--dc21   00-009611

Design:
Elysium, San Francisco, CA

Printed:
Data Reproductions, Auburn Hills, MI

First Printing:
2000
10 9 8 7 6 5 4 3 2 1

Distributed to the trade by:
Publishers Group West

Photographs:
Cover: © Lee Tanner / The Jazz Image
Frontispiece: © Jay Maisel Photography
Back Cover: © Cecco Maino

table of contents

preface

CHET BAKER IS THE SUBJECT of many
misunderstandings. Read anything about Chet Baker—
an article in a magazine or a newspaper, for example
—and it is likely you will be told that Chet was a pitiful
character who started using drugs when his popularity
dwindled and his piano player Dick Twardzik died. That
he faded into obscurity after spectacular early success
and was rescued from oblivion by filmmaker Bruce
Weber, who also inspired his last recording, the soundtrack for *Let's Get Lost*. That he was killed in Amsterdam,
where the police handled the case carelessly.

The truth, alas, is less sensational. Chet had his problems, but he was hardly that badly off. He started using
drugs when he was at the height of his popularity and
Twardzik was still alive. In the last ten years of his life,
he was very popular in Europe, where he recorded and
performed extensively. His trumpet playing was usually
much stronger than it is in Weber's film. The soundtrack
was certainly not his last recording; he made over a
dozen records afterward, both live and in the studio. One
of them—*Chet Baker in Tokyo*—contains his best work
ever. And, finally, Chet was not killed. After thorough
examination, the police concluded that he died because
he fell out of his hotel room, after having taken heroin

and cocaine. This may sound anti-climactic for a jazz hero, but there is nothing I can do about it.

I found out this—and other things—while talking to friends, colleagues and a police sergeant, spending quite some time in libraries, reviewing paper clippings from all parts of the world, and collecting as many recordings as I could. I couldn't have written this book without all those interesting conversations with Chet's widow Carol Baker, his tour manager and troubleshooter Peter Huijts, police sergeant R. Bloos, piano player Russ Freeman, his fellow trumpet player and landlord Evert Hekkema, and his manager Wim Wigt. I also talked to Jasper Blom, Max Bolleman, Philip Catherine, Maarten Derksen, Teddy Edwards, Harry Emmery, John Engels, Herb Geller, Jimmy Heath, Jarmo Hoogendijk, Eric Ineke, Rocky Knauer, Jimmy Knepper, Lee Konitz, Red Mitchell[†], Edu Ninck Blok, Jacques Pelzer[†], Ack van Rooyen, Bud Shank, Gerrie Teekens, and Ria Wigt. I owe especial thanks to Annemieke Claassens, Jacqueline van Hattum, Peter Kok, Tom Mandersloot, the Nationaal Jazz Archief, Klaus Gottwald, Mike Zwerin, Thorbjørn Sjøgren, Hans Henrik Lerfeldt[†], and Bob Hagen. Thanks also to Lee Tanner, Bruce Louden, and Harvey Bloomfield; as well as Terri Hinte of Fantasy Records and Tom Evered of Blue Note/Capitol.

I trust this book will bring readers closer to the appreciation of the man's life and music.

Jeroen de Valk,
Amersfoort, The Netherlands, April 2000

chronology

1929   Born Chesney Henry Baker Jr. on December 23 in Yale, Oklahoma.

1942   Begins to teach himself the trumpet.

1946   Starts playing in army bands.

1950   Marries Charlaine.

1951   Starts working as a full-time jazz musician in California.

1952   On tour with Charlie Parker. Joins the Gerry Mulligan Quartet. First studio recordings, national successes.

1953   On the road with his own quartet, featuring Russ Freeman. Wins several polls, gains popularity as a singer as well.

1955   Goes on a lengthy tour of Europe. His pianist Dick Twardzik dies in Paris.

1956   Back in the USA. Marries Halema. In prison for possession of hard drugs.

1957   His son Chesney is born.

1959   Back to Europe after another prison sentence.

1960   Meets Carol Jackson.

1960   In an Italian prison for sixteen months because of several drug-related offences.

1961   Released from prison. Wanders around Europe, is banned from several countries.

1962   Son Dean (by Carol) is born.

1964   Switches to flugelhorn. Returns to New York with Carol and Dean. Marries Carol.

1965   Starts making a series of commercial recordings with The Mariachi Brass *et al.* Performs sporadically. Son Paul is born.

1966   Loses part of one front tooth in a physical attack, but continues playing. Daughter Melissa ('Missy') is born.

1968   Returns to the trumpet.

c. 1969   Starts wearing dentures. Virtually stops playing professionally. Meets Diane Vavra but is still married to Carol.

1973   Begins a gradual comeback. Meets Ruth Young in New York.

1974   Starts recording again, with Gerry Mulligan (among others).

1975   Tours Europe and takes Ruth Young with him. Does not live with Carol or any of his children anymore.

1978   Back to Europe, where he works most of the time for the rest of his life with diverse artists. Has no fixed address; lives with friends and in hotels. Diane is usually his companion. Records and performs extensively.

1983   After a problematic tour with Stan Getz, starts working with impresario Wim Wigt and Wigt's associate Peter Huijts.

1987   Makes one of his best recordings ever in Tokyo.

1988   Dies on May 13, 58 years old, in Amsterdam, as a result of a fall or jump from his hotel window after having taken a quantity of heroin and cocaine.

a routine burial:
chet baker's death

*P*eter Huijts, Chet Baker's tour manager in Europe and Japan, called it "a wretched funeral." Almost no one had come except a few family members. The trumpeter Jack Sheldon, supposedly a "very good friend," was conspicuously absent. Huijts: "He had promised to play 'My Funny Valentine,' but he had a little gig somewhere else." Of the old friends only Russ Freeman had taken the trouble to drive to Inglewood Cemetery outside Los Angeles. True, Christopher Mason had come—an obscure saxophonist, whose good fortune it was to have nabbed Chet two years earlier for an album of Christmas carols. Now he came to help promote this silly Christmas album.

According to Huijts [pronounced HOYTS], the family did not appear emotionally involved in the ceremony at all. Chet's third wife Carol Baker, their three children, and his second wife Halema, who had stuck with him while he was in prison—all stood there with a neutral expression. His eldest son and namesake Chesney, by Halema, stayed away.

Chet Baker, the trumpeter and singer, who had created

such intense, poignant music in the last ten years of his life, enjoyed little prestige in America. Not much of the music that he made since his final move to Europe in 1978 made an impact here. Of course, the fault was partly his own. He was inept at public relations. He often arrived late to his shows in New York, in bad shape—or not at all. For fourteen years his family saw barely a penny of all the money he earned. He no longer took care of his children's education. He was a master spendthrift. In his final years his manager Wim Wigt paid him at least $1000 a concert, and $5000 per record. Such sums sufficed him only a few days. If Chet visited his family once a year, he was as burned out as ever. Evert Hekkema: "Chet did nothing but tour. He had no home, not even a bank account. I always called him the high-class hobo."

Chet's death on May 13, 1988 in Amsterdam after falling or jumping from a hotel window caused not only consternation but also bewilderment and scandal. It was twelve hours before the "approximately thirty-year-old man" (as he was described in the initial police report) was identified as the 58-year-old Chet Baker. In countless articles Baker's drug addiction was publicized as if it alone were responsible for his fame.

Chet had taken the train to Amsterdam that Thursday, May 12, in the afternoon. He was in a rather bad way, because he had not gotten a fix since Tuesday night–Wednesday morning. In Rotterdam, he had spent a night in the house of Robert van der Feyst, who at the time was also hosting the trumpeter Woody Shaw. Van der Feyst had tried to cop something for Baker, but

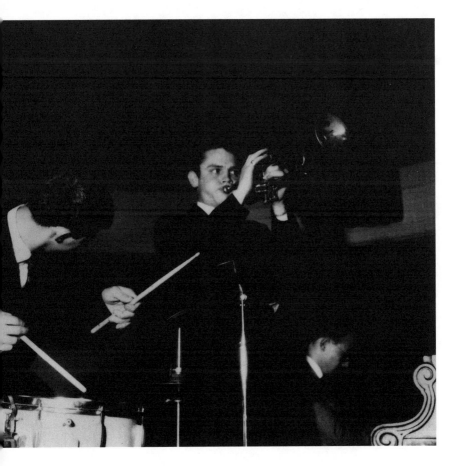

Concert at Teatro Cherubini, Florence, Italy, January 1956. Charles Saudrais, Chet and F. Boland.

© Cecco Maino

without success. Chet went directly from Amsterdam's main train station to the Zeedijk section, where there was always something to be had. He bought not only heroin but also cocaine. After so long a wait, he figured he deserved something extra.

After scoring, he looked for a hotel. After a brief search, he checked into the Prins Hendrik Hotel in the early evening. Usually when he was in the area he stayed at the posher Barbizon Palace or Victoria Hotel on the

Damrak. But it was Ascension Day, the city was packed, and so he was probably content with less deluxe accommodations. He took a room on the third floor, number C-20.

In the evening, he was expected at a concert hall in Laren, where he was scheduled to take part in a celebration of the fifteenth anniversary of the radio program *Sesjun* along with Archie Shepp. Just before leaving for Amsterdam Peter Huijts had called in order to talk to him about the evening. Huijts wanted to have him picked up at seven o'clock at the Memphis Hotel near the Concertgebouw. There Wim Wigt, his manager [pronounced as spelled, except the Ws like Vs], had reserved a room for him. Chet was barely responsive, and it was all Huijts could do just to convey this simple message. Huijts gave Baker his private number as well as the number of the hotel in case there were any problems.

When Wigt's assistant reported at the Memphis Hotel that evening, there was no trace of Chet. The program later that evening started without him. Since the trumpeter was a no-show often enough, his absence elicited no great concern.

That evening, Chet had taken the drugs that he had needed so badly. At a certain point, he apparently wanted to open the window. Presumably, he wanted a little fresh air. The night was warm. The sill was knee-high. The antique sash only went up after many attempts to open it. The wood was old and had been painted over innumerable times. The window would only go up about two feet. It was therefore impossible to sit on the sill comfortably.

CRIMINAL INSPECTOR R. BLOOS: "Baker fell or jumped around 3 in the morning. How did it happen? He was naturally intoxicated from the drugs. Heroin puts you into a kind of half-conscious state. Maybe he suddenly had the delusion he could fly."

The window could be held up with a metal peg that had to be stuck in the window frame. To keep this peg from getting lost, it was fastened to the wall with a small chain. It is probable that, while losing his balance, Chet grabbed the chain. The peg with a part of the broken chain was found beside him on the street. The window fell shut.

BLOOS: "Baker fell on some stone posts with the back of his head. Officially, he died of brain injury. Passers-by saw him lying and thought: he's drunk. His head started to bleed. Somebody noticed and knocked at the hotel door. Nobody in the hotel would open. They probably thought, 'If it is a hotel guest, he has a key, and if it isn't a hotel guest, it's no business of ours.' Then somebody went into a Surinamese bar on the Zeedijk and reported that there was a man lying in the street, either drunk or possibly injured. The police were called. The official report refers to 'a man approximately thirty years old.' One must take into account that it was night, the deceased was a slight man, and his face was covered in blood."

The door to his room was locked from the inside. The police ruled out foul play. It is true that somebody could have opened the door from the outside with the hotel's master key, but there was no sign of a struggle.

Conversely, there was the distinct imprint of his trousers in the dust on the sill, which would surely have been smeared had Chet been pushed from the window. He had lain or sat there some time, had straightened up, and either fell or jumped. [On page 193ff further details concerning Baker's death will be found.]

INSPECTOR BLOOS: "From the needle tracks and from what my colleagues found in the room, it soon became clear that we were dealing with a drug addict. I come into the office, see the report and think: A thirty-year-old addict with the papers of an American almost sixty years old—this must be a junkie who has robbed a tourist. And it happens often enough that a junkie registers in a hotel under an assumed name. In the hotel register he had written the address of a Mr. Baker of Yale, Oklahoma. I immediately sent a telex to Yale asking whether anyone knew of any theft that had taken place there."

PETER HUIJTS: "Wim Wigt, his wife Ria, and I started the search towards midnight. We called hospitals, police stations. Not with all the details, because you don't want to just set the police on the guy. I still remember the next day exactly. It was a Friday. In the morning I had done some shopping. I came home at noon and thought: Something isn't right. Then I called the police. With the whole story, what I thought and believed, and who it was about. After some back and forth, the officer suddenly thought of something, and told me a very strange story. They had found a man about thirty years old—they didn't tell me yet that he was dead—with a trumpet in his possession. I said, 'Damn, that can't be him, because he was much older. But if you found a trumpet, that could be his, and since there are problems, I am coming to Amsterdam anyway.' 'But before you come, we have to tell you something. The man is dead.' Then they said something about a pair of glasses they had found—horn-glasses of a kind Chet sometimes wore—and about a passport.

"The police showed no great eagerness to get to the bottom of the matter. As far as they were concerned, they had just found another junkie in the street. I already realized that. I waited two hours in the police station in the Warmoesstraat and thought: No wonder it's going like this—it's extremely busy around here. They had laid him out and simply waited until some information about him came through. They had hardly taken the time to investigate. In the open trumpet case lay a piece of paper with my telephone number and that of the Memphis Hotel, and another telex from Wim Wigt. These they had completely overlooked.

"Two persons had to be present at the identification. My wife said, 'I'll come, and I want to drive, because you're much too upset.' We went to the police station and then to a room at the Westgaarde cemetery, where he was laid out. In the station, it already became as good as certain that it would be Chet. But with him you never knew . . .

"I thought: 'It's going to be horrible to see him. The poor guy has fallen out the window.' But in fact he looked quite uninjured because he had landed on the back of his head. We still had to discuss whether the coffin should be open or closed. In the meantime so many rumors were circulating that he was nothing but a disfigured mass that it was decided to leave it open. Nobody there knew who Chet Baker was. I said to the police officers, 'There are certainly going to be people from the press coming to see you.' They shot me a look as if to say, He's certainly putting on airs. Next day, though, they called me: they were going crazy from all the telephone calls. Then it finally became clear to them that they were dealing with someone besides a common junkie."

Evert Hekkema: "When Chet died, we said: 'He should go into the coffin with a T-shirt and jeans.' Because that's how he always dressed. But family members had arranged that he would be buried the way he looked in the '60s: in a neat suit and tie. Peter called me and gave me the order to lay him out for the wake. He said, 'Try to do something that is acceptable for them as well as us.' So I bought a light gray double-breasted suit with four buttons. The idea was that the jacket would not just fall open when lying flat; it would hold its shape. You can fold the lapels of the jacket over each other. I also bought a violet silk tie to go with it. I myself also had a tiepin with a trumpet, which I sometimes wore. I had the funeral director put it on the tie.

"On May 18 in Amsterdam we took our leave of Chet. A whole crowd of musicians, friends and fans had come. I had not seen him in a year and a half. He lay there quite peacefully as if he were sleeping. The funeral home had really pieced him together. But I cast a glance into the coffin, and that was already too much for me."

More important than Chet's death, though, is his music.

One could divide his career into two parts: the period before his comeback in 1974, and the years following. For many jazz writers, only the first period counts. European lovers of jazz look at it differently. From 1974 on Chet achieved an intensity unmatched by just about any other jazz musician.

I saw him countless times: sitting hunched in a chair, his trumpet at knee height, the horn very close to the microphone. He had a veiled, tender sound that seemed to come not from a trumpet but a flugelhorn. He was a relic of bygone times. Expressivity was foremost; his technique and grasp of theory were rudimentary. At a concert in 1985 at Amsterdam's Bimhuis, I heard nothing from conservatory students but negative remarks about his lack of technique and the murmur that passed for his singing. In his last years, he played with an effort and a dedication like no other. He turned his heart inside out so that listeners became almost embarrassed listening to him. One still has the same experience listening to his better records. In the '70s something peculiar happened with his tone. In this respect he can be compared with no one else, not even Miles Davis. He blew very softly, with a crystal-clear base and no vibrato. It was a flawless sound, with many undertones. Chet had little high end, but what he lacked at the top he made up for in the bottom. He had a splendid sound in the deepest register because his lips were so relaxed when he played. As Evert Hekkema remarked, "Chet plays on average a half octave lower than the average jazz trumpeter."

Chet gave the impression that he played each note at exactly the right moment, and that each note followed inevitably on the preceding one—on a good day. For there is another side to the coin: Chet was one of the least consistent artists in jazz history. When he was in good form, he surpassed, in my opinion, every other living jazz musician. When he wasn't, though—and such days were not infrequent—then he could barely produce a note. At such times—collapsed like a folding chair and staring blankly in front of him—he was a needlessly cruel parody of himself.

In this book, I will try and throw some light on the personality of Chet Baker. That is not easy. Chet was quiet and introverted. He could win people over easily, but essentially this 'high-class hobo' had a close relationship with nothing but music and drugs. Hekkema: "Chet was usually in a melancholy mood. A depressive guy. He had seen how time turned against him. In his early 20s he blazed forth like a comet. Everyone idolized him; nothing stood in his way. That had consequences for the remainder of his life. His popularity dwindled, but Chet didn't change. He had absolutely no sense of responsibility.

"His playing had something effortless about it. He never thought, Can I reach this high note? or, What is the name of this chord? The strain every other trumpeter has to contend with was unknown to him. He kept his boyish innocence, which was the source of his charm. In the '60s, when he had already been through so much, he still sang like a sixteen-year-old boy. He looked like one too. And the remainder of his life he passed in a dream, like an adolescent."

Peter Huijts: "He was always on the lookout for kicks. It

seemed like he was never satisfied. He did the strangest things. Once, he was sailing in America with his girl-friend Diane. The boat capsized, and the pair of them sat twelve long hours in the capsized boat. That's the sort of thing that happened to him. Once he showed up at the airport with a brick-red face, completely swollen. I said, 'What the hell happened to you?' He had bought a motorcycle and had raced it through the California desert. Without any protection against the sun. Of course he then lost the motorcycle somewhere. In Japan, we once went for a walk on the beach. Suddenly Chet said that he wanted to buy or rent a motorcycle, to tear around the beach in. But none could be found. So then he was immediately in a foul mood. He couldn't stand that. He could not deal with such small setbacks."

In 1975 Chet left his third wife Carol and their children. After that, he led an inconstant existence, which after 1978 passed mainly in Europe. He sometimes let it be known that he wanted to start a new life, but couldn't take the necessary steps. For those who knew him, his death came as no great surprise.

Peter Huijts: "Something had to happen sooner or later. Things couldn't go on as they were, he knew that him-self. Sometimes he had fantasies of a little house with garden, settling down, playing a concert here and there. He often spoke of buying or renting an apartment. But it came to nothing. For someone with his lifestyle, his addiction, something like that is very hard. Even the first steps in that direction were all but impossible. He could barely make resolutions. In his clear moments, he could visualize what he wanted. But when it came to really undertaking something, then nothing came to pass. One never got to know him well enough to find out what he was really feeling. I had very extensive contact with Chet, but where personal issues were involved, he never revealed himself."

Carol Baker: "In the last five years of his life Chet visited his family more frequently. About two, sometimes three times a year. It slowly became clear to him that he had lost contact with his children. In a couple of particular years, he had heard nothing from them at all. Suddenly he wanted to make up for it. He realized that, from being a good family father he had turned into a bum. His life was one big mess. He said that he wanted to change everything again. But those were utopias. They were dreams."

"I saw him for the last time in 1987. He said I had to go to Europe with him. That he would buy a house for us there and everything would be fine. 'Let's go back together to Europe. We'll buy a house, live together, and you won't have to work any more.' He embarrassed me that way. I didn't dare hurt his feelings. I didn't want to say no directly. But I couldn't any more. My life had changed. I had lived alone almost fifteen years by that time. Our children had grown up here; I had my work here. I was a secretary with the head of the engineering program at Oklahoma State University. I said, 'Chet, I don't speak a word of French, what will I do there?' And the musician life is not for me—late to bed, hanging out in smoky clubs . . .' "

The Dutch drummer Eric Ineke: "I played with Chet only once. But I still remember it precisely. It was November 9, 1979. We were supposed to record a few numbers in the studio for the jazz program on station KRO. It was scheduled to start at seven o'clock. Of course, I was there well ahead of time, in order to put my kit together. Chet was nowhere to be found. I believe he only arrived sometime after seven. Everyone had gotten anxious by that time. 'Hello,' he said amiably, as if everything were fine, 'here I am. I hope you aren't mad at me, but I lost my music somewhere.' He had also lost the parts for the accompanists. He sat down at the piano and started to play with one hand. 'Do you know "Lucius Lou"?,' he asked Frans Elsen, the pianist. No, Frans didn't know that one. 'It goes something like this,' Chet said, and began to hunt for the notes, completely in silence. 'It goes this way (*plink plink*), then like this (*plink plink*)— no, like this, I think,' and so on. He was in no hurry at all. Frans sat alongside him and tried to help. Did Chet want this chord or that? That wasn't easy, because Chet wanted things in a definite way but couldn't explain clearly what that was, since he had no notion of chords. He always played by ear. I quietly tried playing along. 'No, not like that,' he said after a few bars. He took one of my sticks and beat out a certain rhythm on the cymbal. 'It has to be this way.' That's when I realized: This was going to be a long session.

"After three quarters of an hour we started the first take. Then Chet said that he wanted to play 'Candy.' He sat himself down at the piano, and again began to tinkle with one hand—completely calm, as if there were no studio, no producer. And on it went. For each piece, we needed three quarters of an hour to rehearse.

"Finally he asked me what time it was. 'Eleven,' I said. 'How many numbers have we recorded?' 'Four,' I said. 'Four,' Chet repeated, and mused on it as if the number pleased him. 'Well, four pieces is enough for a jazz program,' he said. And with that he packed his trumpet into its case. Edwin Rutten, the producer, was completely beside himself. There were only twenty minutes of music on tape! Then Chet said something that I will never forget. 'I'm sorry, man. I sold you my time and my talent.' He shook the musicians' hands, said that it had been tremendous fun for him, took the full payment, and disappeared into the darkness. Only in recent weeks, nearly ten years later, have I heard the recordings. Frans Elsen gave me a tape. It sounds fantastic. Chet sang and played superbly."

a cowboy from oklahoma: chet's early years

*a*fter 1975, Chet no longer had a permanent residence. But situations would regularly arise—like when checking into a hotel—that he had to state an address. Then he would always put Yale, Oklahoma—the city where he was born Chesney Henry Baker on December 23, 1929.

In the opinion of the German-Canadian bass player Rocky Knauer, Chet always remained 'a cowboy from Oklahoma'. "He always made cynical comments. Once we were in the north of Sweden. In the summer there it is fifty during the day and nearly freezing at night. Chet ran around as usual in jeans and a T-shirt. He never complained of the cold. And whenever Chet was challenged, he could be pretty aggressive. He was tough!"

Chet was born on a farm on the outskirts of Yale; his mother, Vera Baker, *née* Moser, had come into the world there herself. Peter Huijts met Chet's mother in California at her son's funeral. "She told me that Chet had caused her a lot of grief." Chet remained close to his mother all his life. During the years he could not perform in public (around 1968–1973), he moved back in with her along with his own family. In later years he continued to see her often. Vera Baker is a small, friendly woman with a round, friendly face; she is 90 now and lives in a rest home in Yale. The only photo of Chet's father, Chesney Henry Baker, Sr., that I have seen dates from 1947.* Chet Senior was a big, wiry man with crow's-feet eyes; in the picture he towers over his wife by more than a head. He is lean, but doesn't radiate the vulnerability that his son did. With his stern gaze, he reminds one a little of Clint Eastwood. Chet Sr. died in 1967. Vera Baker worked in the city in a perfumery, while Chet Sr. tried to make a living as a musician. He was a jazz fan and played banjo, later guitar. To get by he worked as a singer and guitarist in a country-and-western outfit that played every morning at six o'clock on a local radio station. Among Chet's earliest memories is the theme song his father sang on the air: "I'm an Old Cowhand from the Rio Grande." Chet could reproduce some of this sentimental tune later, though he denied that country and western had an influence on his own playing; in fact, he said he detested the music. Maarten Derksen, a colleague of Wim Wigt: "Chet told me that his father played western swing, a kind of jazzy country and western. The music resembled a little that of the Hot Club of France. 'That was as far as dad could go,' he said. Chet also said that he himself sang on the radio with his father's band." Chet in an interview with the French magazine *Jazz Hot* (November 1983): "My father was a good musician. He had a good ear and good timing."

*It appears in *Let's Get Lost, A Film Journal by Bruce Weber* (Little Bear Films, 1988).

Earnings for a musician were not exactly abundant in the years of the depression. So in 1930, when Chet was one, his father moved the family in with his sister Agnes in Oklahoma City. Summers they spent back in Yale. "Every summer I'd spend a couple of months on the farm in Yale walking the dirt road that led to the highway, picking wild raspberries along the way. Often I'd walk out into the watermelons, pick one up over my head, and let it fall so that it split wide open. Then I'd eat the sweet heart out of it and leave the rest to the birds."*

In 1940—Chet was now ten—his father joined many Okies in moving the family to California. Glendale, north of LA, was then a small industrial city, and Chet Sr. got a job there in a Lockheed factory. According to Carol, Chet Sr. no longer picked up his guitar after the move to California.

Chet had no brothers or sisters. He was an only child and got a lot of attention from his mother. Carol Baker: "Chet was an only child, and a spoiled child. His mother spoiled him completely! She did everything for him. Until the end of his life, she treated him like a ten-year-old. Whenever Chet came to visit, she said, 'Chet, you need a haircut. Chet, you look terrible. Chet, why don't you wear something decent for once?' They never realized that one day he had to become a grown-up man. He visited once every year. He became old and wrinkled, but their relationship to him didn't change a bit. 'Chet, you have to eat more. And can't you wash your pants just once?' 'Yes, mother,' he would groan. He could never stand it with them more than a week."

*Chet Baker, As though I had wings: the lost memoir (New York 1997), 21

Chet's parents promoted his musical abilities as well as they could. On Sunday afternoons, his mother dragged him to amateur competitions. There, he had to share the stage with children who step-danced, played the accordion, or performed other little novelty acts. At eleven or twelve he sang, not children's songs, but popular songs like "Old Devil Moon" or "I Had the Craziest Dream"— not exactly the repertoire one expects from a boy his age. He never got first prize, but once he got second. At this time he was also singing in a church choir.

Carol Baker: "Chet's father was a big fan of Jack Teagarden. Although they had little money, he managed to get hold of a trombone for his son. But Chet, who was twelve at that time, couldn't do anything with it. He was still too small. He found it a big clumsy thing, and his arms were so short that he couldn't move the slide properly. The trombone disappeared, and a few weeks later, on Chet's thirteenth birthday, his father bought him a trumpet." Vera Baker told the filmmaker Bruce Weber in 1987: "His father wanted him to be just a natural musician, but his father really held reins on him. I don't think they were so close. I think he was closer to me. He was just exactly like his father. We lived in Oklahoma City with his aunt and uncle. They had a radio and we only had popular music on for one hour in the day and when it was on he would climb up on the stool and just sit there for one hour and listen. And when it was through playing he would just climb down, and be real quiet for a while, and then start playing. He learned songs by memory when he was that young. Yes, he didn't get a trumpet until he was about eleven. And his father bought it at a pawn shop, and he just brought it home and sat it down and didn't say, 'Chet, this is yours,' so Chet just took it and started practicing and listening to records. And in two weeks he was picking out 'The Two O'Clock Jump' by Harry James."

As a trumpeter, Chet remained an autodidact his whole life. He attended the instrument training class at his junior high school for a time, but didn't learn much, because he relied almost wholly on his ear. He played the repertoire of the school orchestra—marches and hits of the day—without glancing at the music. He did learn to read a little at the time—not much, but together with what he later learned in army bands, enough to get by during recording sessions. But arrangers always had to allow for his limitations.

Chet's notorious mouth problems began early. He had been playing the trumpet only six months when he was hit in the mouth by a rock thrown by a schoolmate. As a result, he lost his upper left front tooth. This forced him to alter his technique, and he was limited in his ability to play loud and high. Up until around 1968, when he got an artificial denture, he had to manage without one of his incisors, which are critical for trumpet technique. In photos he is usually seen holding his mouth carefully closed.

Chet was not a brilliant student. He didn't lack intelligence, only application. Carol Baker: "He was bored. And he wanted to get away from what I would call the smothering embrace of his mother. And so already at the age of sixteen he joined the army. That was apparently the only chance he had at the time to become a little independent. Soon he was assigned to a military band in Germany."

In his brief memoir he writes: "I became disenchanted with school during my junior year at Redondo High. I cut lots of classes and spent nearly every day on the beach or along the cliffs of Palos Verdes diving for abalone. My truancy didn't sit too well with my folks; we had a few family discussions about it, and finally I decided to join the Army" (As though I had wings, 22–23).

When Chet reported to the military, he said that he was seventeen so that the recruitment office would admit him. At first he was assigned an office job, but after a short time was enlisted in the 298th Army Band, stationed at the time in Berlin. He remained there a year. By his own account, only now did he start to get really interested in jazz. Previously, Harry James had been the only jazz trumpeter he knew. The tenor saxophonist Teddy Edwards, who lived in California in the '50s, claims that he heard Chet already playing jazz as a fifteen-year-old. It is possible, however, that Edward was misled by his youthful appearance as to Chet's true age.

Critics compare the early Chet Baker with Bix Beiderbecke and Bobby Hackett. Even if there are similarities between these white trumpeters, there can be no question of influence. Chet was already a fan of contemporary bebop and took no interest in older jazz. "I never heard that much about Bix . . . Bobby Hackett doesn't go far enough for me. He plays the melody very nicely, but there was not much real improvisation in his playing . . . If I had to play that way every night, I would die of boredom inside of a month" (*The Wire*, November 1985.)

In Berlin he heard V-discs. These were records produced especially for American soldiers who after World War II were stationed all over the world. (V stands for Victory). The first V-Discs that he got to hear over the Armed Forces Network were from Dizzy Gillespie and Stan Kenton. Chet said in interviews later that Dizzy was probably his first influence. He called his first introduction to modern jazz a 'rude awakening': "From Harry James to Dizzy Gillespie is kind of a big jump, you know" [from *Let's Get Lost*].

In 1948, Chet was released from the army and returned to California. Apparently he was aware that his education was somewhat deficient, because he signed up for harmony and theory classes at El Camino College in LA. But he didn't manage to complete the courses. He was too busy getting to know jazz at first hand, specifically the jazz scene of LA. Among the trumpeters in the area who attracted his attention were the brothers Conte and Pete Candoli, and the lesser known Kenny Bright.

Chet ran from one jam session to the next. He also played in Roy Porter's big band, where he could measure his strengths against that of other ambitious young musicians on the West Coast. Eric Dolphy, Jimmy Knepper, Art Farmer and Teddy Edwards were among those who played in this outfit between 1948 and 1950.

In 1950 Chet got married for the first time. "One day I spotted this beautiful blonde sitting at the [Lighthouse] bar. I had seen her a couple of times before and had told myself that I would hit on her if she came in again. When the set broke, I worked my way through the packed club until I was beside her. I can't remember what I said exactly, but within half an hour we were parked in her father's new Buick along the cliffs of Palos Verdes" (*As though I had wings*, 37). Carol Baker: "Chet's first wife was named Charlaine. She worked in a clothing business. Chet was twenty; she was a few years older. They had met on Hermosa Beach when he played there in the Lighthouse club. Shortly after that they got married. The marriage didn't last long. Chet always claimed that they would have split up, because she had had a thing with his lawyer. I don't know the details, but she married a lawyer after the divorce, I don't know whether it was the same one. That's all Chet told me. He didn't talk very much about women, he didn't like to gossip. Sometimes he mumbled something like, 'She was a nice girl, but it didn't work out too well for the two of us.' "

Like a lot of youthful relationships, it seemed to be based on sex. "She loved to be screwed and I loved screwing her" [*Ibid.*]. According to pianist Russ Freeman, "Chet had wandering eyes. He fooled around with other girls all the time." According to Chet: "I really had it bad for Charlaine, but I wasn't alone. There was another dude who also liked her action. Charlaine and I eventually argued over this and some other stuff, and because of it I re-enlisted directly into the Sixth Army Band up in San Francisco, a three-year commitment."

Chet's decision to re-up was motivated not only by personal, but financial considerations. For one year his life had the following routine: During the day he plays in the Presidio Army Band in San Francisco. Then he gets some rest, gets up around midnight, goes to a jam session—and is careful to be back in time to blow reveille at six the next morning. Six months into his second stint in the army he and Charlaine reconciled, and the couple got hitched in Las Vegas, while Chet was on a three-day pass.

Charlaine later married twice more. At the time of Chet's death, she was called Charlaine Voorheis and still lived in California. She died there herself two years later, in 1990.

Towards the end of 1951, after Chet had led this double-life a year, he was transferred to Fort Huachuka. The fort lies in the middle of the Arizona desert—the nearest town is seventy miles away. No jazz, no pretty girls, no music except marches and the daily reveille. "There I was, plucked out of my comfortable S.F. routine and separated from my wife, plopped down out in the middle of nowhere. I hung on for about sixty days, but finally I couldn't stand it anymore and I went AWOL" [*Ibid.*, 43]. Chet returned to LA to spend an idyllic month with Charlaine, but eventually resolved to report back to his unit in San Francisco. At first he was put in the stockade, then transferred to the psych ward. Three weeks later, to his great relief, he received a general discharge, meaning that he was judged 'unadaptable to Army life.'

After saying his final farewell to military bands, Chet

began to work in Los Angeles as a freelance musician. He got back together with Charlaine, who kept her position in the clothing business so that he could perform. Chet in *Let's Get Lost*: "One of my first jobs was with [tenor player] Vido Musso. You probably don't remember him . . . He made one record of *Come Back to Sorrento*, with Stan Kenton, and it was such a big hit that he was able to be booked and have his own group, and the drummer got me on the band."

Chet's earliest recordings date from March 24, 1952. Somebody left their tape recorder on while Chet jammed with the saxophonists Sonny Criss and Wardell Gray, and some others [*Chet Baker Live at The Trade Winds* (Fresh Sound FSCD 1001)]. During this same period he also played with the Stan Getz group.

Not long afterward Chet got his Big Break. He received a telegram from his friend Dick Bock with the news that Charlie Parker was holding an audition at three o'clock that same afternoon in the Tiffany Club. (Bock, still a student at the time, would later become famous as the producer of Pacific Jazz Records.) Chet related his version of the story to nearly every interviewer. It goes like this: In the dim club Parker was trying out a couple of trumpeters. Chet enters, and when his eyes have adjusted to the dark, he sees that just about every trumpeter in LA has shown up. Parker, who has heard about Chet, asks whether he is there too. Chet introduces himself, steps on the stage—and after two numbers, Parker announces that the audition is over. Chet has the job. Later, when back in New York, Parker would tell all the trumpeters: "There's a little white cat on the coast who's gonna eat you up."

In concert with Parker.

© William Claxton

Is this how it actually happened? The record of a concert of Parker with Chet in June of 1952 offers little in the way of exciting trumpet playing [*Bird and Chet* (Fresh Sound FSR CD 17)]. Chet has pretty ideas, but his technique is undeveloped, and his sound is mediocre. If his version of events is true, it shows at least that Parker was capable of recognizing talent in its infancy. After all, Miles, too, was hardly a star when he played with Parker in 1945 as a nineteen-year-old.

Parker was exactly 31 at that time, but looked a lot older. He had been a professional for fifteen years already. He drank great quantities of cognac and took all manner of drugs. But he took the trouble to keep Chet away from the dealers who constantly hung around. Chet had good memories of the weeks he spent with Parker. The altoist always appeared promptly on the stage, played well— and, because he was pleased with his sidemen, persuaded the club owner to pay them 25 dollars a head extra. The fact that Chet was sometimes the only white guy in the group caused—at least for Parker—no problems. Parker even jammed once after a concert with a country-and-western band.

Parker and Chet appeared together for the first time on May 29, 1952, at the Tiffany Club in Los Angeles. Among other engagements, there followed two benefit concerts for television on behalf of muscular dystrophy, and a week at the Say When Club in San Francisco. This gig came to a sudden end when Parker announced that there was going to be a mandatory collection in the club for muscular dystrophy, and that the club owner was going to match whatever the club's patrons kicked in.

The owner refused, whereat Parker took the microphone and publicly denounced the owner as 'cheap.' He and his quintet were fired on the spot. And with this incident, Chet's baptism by fire was complete.

the pianoless quartet:
chet, mulligan and
the west coast scene

*I*n 1952, a tall, skinny young man arrived in Los Angeles—Gerry Mulligan. He was 25 years old (born April 6, 1927), by profession an arranger. He also played saxophone. Among musicians he had a good reputation, mainly owing to his arrangements for the short-lived Miles Davis nonet. Admittedly, this alone could not get him far, and he also had a drug problem. He had hitch-hiked from New York to LA in hopes that life there would be more congenial. Shortly after his arrival, he succeeded in peddling a few arrangements to Stan Kenton. And he participated in the marathon jam sessions—from 2 in the afternoon until 2 at night!—in the Lighthouse (the aforementioned club in the nearby resort town of Hermosa Beach).

In the summer of that same year, Mulligan got a regular gig in The Haig, a small club—actually a renovated bungalow—on Wilshire Boulevard with room for 85 patrons. Dick Bock persuaded the owner John Bennett to host a jam session Monday evenings, when the house band was off. In order to appeal to the public, a soloist had to be added, and through Bock's intercession, Mulligan got the job. Al Haig played piano during the breaks.

Gerry Mulligan.
© Paul J. Hoeffler

Los Angeles had many jam sessions in this era. They mostly took place when musicians had some free time—at night, after work, on Sunday afternoon or Monday night. A few musicians—mainly drummers, pianists and bass players—got paid eight or ten dollars, the others played for the hell of it.

Among the regular guests at the Haig were alto saxo-
phonist Sonny Criss, trumpeter Ernie Royal, the pianists
Jimmy Rowles and Fred Otis, bass players Joe Comfort,
Red Mitchell, and Joe Mondragon, and drummers Chico
Hamilton and Alvin Stoller.

On June 16, 1952, Chet and Mulligan met in the club.
Mulligan liked Chet's playing, and a few Mondays later
decided to establish a regular quintet with the 22-year-
old trumpeter. (There was apparently no need of the
audition mentioned in some jazz books.) A few weeks
later, on July 9, some regular guests of the Haig met at
the home of the sound technician Phil Turetsky:
Mulligan, Jimmy Rowles, Joe Mondragon—and Chet,
whom Mulligan had invited. The drummer Chico
Hamilton didn't show. They rehearsed a little, then taped
two numbers. Initially only one was released: "She Didn't
Say Yes."* The music appeared on the recently newly
formed Pacific Jazz label. Bock was both manager and
producer. He also took care of distribution in that he visited all the record stores in the area with records loaded
in his own car.

According to Chet, there was also a rehearsal at this time
without piano. This rehearsal could have led to the decision to continue without one. The pianoless approach,
however, also had a very practical basis. The trio of the
vibe player Red Norvo (with guitarist Tal Farlow and
bassist Red Mitchell) had been the featured attraction at
the Haig. This group required no piano, so, to make more
room on the tiny stage, Norvo suggested to the owner
that the piano be put in storage for the time being.

*The Original Gerry Mulligan Quartet with Chet Baker (Mosaic MD3-102)

Mulligan consented. He was anxious not to lose this regular gig since he was living hand to mouth, and he wanted to try playing a little longer without piano anyway. The saxophonist had won the trust of Bennett in the meantime and could appear on Monday nights with his own group. The quartet's rhythm section consisted at first of Chico Hamilton and Bob Whitlock, a young bass player from Long Beach.

In the liner notes to his first LP on Pacific Jazz, Mulligan writes: "I consider the string bass to be the basis of the sound of the group; the foundation on which the soloist builds his line, the main thread around which the two horns weave their contrapuntal interplay. It is possible with two voices to imply the sound of or impart the feeling of any chord or series of chords, as Bach shows us so thoroughly and enjoyably in his inventions. When a piano is used in a group it necessarily plays the dominant role . . . The soloist is forced to adapt his line to the changes and alterations made by the pianist in the chords of the progression."*

The first evenings in which Mulligan and Chet must make do without piano are none too promising. Sometimes the rhythm section played whole choruses alone while the horns stood there wondering what they were supposed to be doing. Things improved, however, and after five Mondays the group was ready to record. In August, they tape the single "Lullaby of the Leaves/ Bernie's Tune" for Pacific Jazz (*The Original Gerry Mulligan Quartet with Chet Baker*). The disk delivered

Gerry Mulligan Quartet (Pacific Jazz PJ LP-1)

With Gerry
Mulligan (bs) and
Lee Konitz (alto),
1953.
© William Claxton

the Mulligan combo as well as Pacific Jazz their first hit, and an engagement in San Francisco's Blackhawk followed in consequence.

The young bass player Bob Whitlock, however, did not yet feel ready for the Big Time and elected to go on to college in Salt Lake City. He was replaced by Carson Smith. With Smith, the quartet did a recording for Fantasy, on which the splendid Mulligan composition "Line for Lyons" and the first version of "My Funny

33

Valentine" were performed (*The Original Gerry Mulligan Quartet with Chet Baker*). In October the group returned to the Haig for a four-week engagement, which was extended again and again. Ultimately it would last six months.

Bock is of the opinion that the success of the Mulligan quartet is partially owed to him. "When we made the first quartet records, [Chet] was still pretty immature," he said later to writer Alun Morgan, "and I had to do a lot of editing and splicing to make complete solos without any fluffs" (*Jazz Monthly*, June 1963). In October another shakeup occurs. Because The Haig is so small, the owner cannot pay much more than the union minimum. Hamilton, by far the oldest member of the group, has a family to support, and therefore cannot pass up a lucrative offer from singer Lena Horne. In Larry Bunker, Mulligan found a suitable replacement on drums.

After their return to the Haig, the Mulligan quartet becomes the nightclub's main attraction. The club is always full, and on weekends, the number waiting outside is bigger than the audience inside—not too surprising, considering that the most popular jazz group in the city is playing in a club with a capacity of exactly 85. Every evening the members of the jet set park their big cars in front of the small club. Movie stars like Jane Russell and Marilyn Monroe come to The Haig in their free hours.

A small incident disturbs the idyll. One evening the contentious Mulligan has the group break off in the middle of a piece to deliver the audience a stern lecture. The problem? Too much conversation is going on during their playing. The press won't let the incident go: such insolence is virtually unheard of at the time. In *Down Beat* (May 20, 1953) Mulligan got the chance to explain himself: "Most of The Haig's customers are there to listen to the music—those who aren't don't matter. It's a small place, and when anyone starts talking it not only annoys those who are trying to listen, but disturbs the continuity of our collective musical thinking. I know the people talk, laugh, and carry on down there at the Lighthouse all the time when Rumsey's band is playing—but they blast all night long anyway, so it doesn't matter." With this last remark Mulligan—no doubt unintentionally—incurred the hostility of the bass player Howard Rumsey and his musicians.*

Much has been written about the interplay of Mulligan and Chet. They understood each other on an almost telepathic level. For some pieces, Mulligan had written out arrangements, but other performances evolved quite spontaneously. Mulligan was awed by his young sideman's natural talent. Chet was never afraid to make a mistake, he simply played what he felt. Mulligan's solos often have an academic flavor —one can hear him deliberately go through the changes—while Chet's solos are drawn from the hesitancy, the experimentation, and the insights of the real improviser. Ten years later, Mulligan told *Down Beat*: "Chet was one of the best intuitive musicians I've ever seen . . . I remember one night at The Haig in Los Angeles, nobody called a tune all evening. As

*See "Mulligan's Blast Was Just an Act," *Down Beat,* June 3, 1953.

a tune ended, someone would noodle another melody, and we would all go into the same thing. We'd play for an hour and a half that way, take a break and go on and do it again. It never let up. It was one of the most exciting evenings of playing I can remember" (*Down Beat*, January 17, 1963).

Alto saxophonist Herb Geller: "Gerry was not available for a few weeks once. I was allowed to stand in for him. It was a big honor to play with the most popular band of Los Angeles. I remember Chet as a friendly, introverted young man and a remarkable musician. He played completely by ear; he never knew what key the pieces were in. So there was no point in asking *him*. He simply played, he had no clue beyond that. Of course I was nervous, I had to stand in suddenly and had no idea what was expected of me. In general, whenever we hit an impasse Larry Bunker would come out from behind his drum set. Larry was a trained musician and played vibraphone too. He would tell us what the key was, what my first note was, what Chet's first note was, which chord the bass player should start with, etc. It sometimes happened that in the middle of a solo Chet would blow a completely wrong note. Then he immediately moved on to the right note and rounded off the phrase so that it sounded wonderful—as if he had planned it that way."

The success of the Gerry Mulligan quartet inaugurated a popular musical style called West Coast Jazz. It is a light-footed 'white' music, that in a certain respect was the dead opposite of the heated hard bop on the East Coast. Herb Geller: "The newspapers printed sensational stories with headlines like 'East Coast vs. West Coast'—as

Jimmy Giuffre,

1956.

© Paul J. Hoeffler

if the musicians of New York and LA were sworn ene-
mies. Nonsense of course, but at least that way we got a
little publicity."

Today, most of the musicians from this period want to hear nothing more about 'West Coast Jazz'. Bud Shank, later a boisterous sax player who would not have been out of place in Art Blakey's Jazz Messengers, insists that the West Coast records were not representative of the playing of the young Californians: "The concepts 'West Coast' and 'East Coast' were invented by some critics from New York. The critics thought that all the groups in California played like the Mulligan Quartet. West Coast Jazz only became a kind of movement when the producers noticed that a certain type of music was marketable. They told the arrangers and bandleaders: 'Do it this way.' Arrangers like Shorty Rogers and Jimmy Giuffre took the young musicians from the area into the studio and said: 'This is West Coast Jazz, and you have to play like this, because it's what people want to hear.' It became a commodity. But what we played in the clubs was completely different, even then. Just listen to the live recordings of the Lighthouse All Stars.*

"A lot of Californian musicians don't like to be reminded of this time. You should know that some of them were still quite young, just out of high school. They went through a whole new development later, but no one knows about it. Everyone is obsessed with the records from the '50s."

This applies to Chet and Mulligan as well. At the time of the quartet, a long evolution lay ahead of both of them. Chet especially would get annoyed later because he was perpetually judged by his earliest recordings.

---

*At Last! Miles Davis and the Lighthouse All Stars (Contemporary F649) and Witch Doctor / Chet Baker and the Lighthouse All Stars (OJC 609)

Bud Shank at
Newport, July
1956.
© Paul J. Hoeffler

The black musicians in California were none too pleased, either, about the popularity of the new West Coast jazz. The tenor saxophonist Teddy Edwards and his hard-swinging music were no longer in style. He still talks with some irritation about this era. "I always say: 'The jazz out of New York was heavy and black and the

Stan Getz on tenor with Frankie Isola on drums, Rochester, NY, 1957.

© Paul J. Hoeffler

jazz out of the west was light and white.' But of course that really only applies to the records. Suddenly there were no more recording dates for black West Coast musicians like Hampton Hawes, Sonny Criss, Wardell Gray, Dexter Gordon, and me. We had no more work. Just because we played powerfully. The West Coast kids were afraid that we would blow them out of the studio.

The Lighthouse? That's me. I was in the original lineup of the Lighthouse All Stars. I was the one that made the Lighthouse successful. Bud Shank was still sitting at home practicing. He didn't once dare unpack his horn when there was a jam session.

"The white musicians played shy and timid in the studios and in the clubs. The only personality among them was Chet Baker. He was unique although he was still a kid. I heard him playing when he still wore short pants—short khaki pants all the time. He was a teenager and already he played everywhere. I also saw him appearing at that time with Stan Getz. Stan was seventeen. Chet already played exactly the way he did later. The same pretty sound. He always had a splendid sound. I liked his playing much better than that of the other so-called West Coast players.

"I will tell you something else. Mulligan owes his success to Chet. Gerry made a lot of money with the songs that Chet already played for years, like 'My Funny Valentine' and 'Bernie's Tune.' Chet was playing them way before he met Gerry. Besides him there were few trumpeters who had something to say. Yes, there was Shorty Rogers, but besides him I can't think of anyone. And Shorty also turned away from the black musicians. Gene Norman of the label Gene Norman Presents said to me: 'Why don't you do a record with Shorty?' So I said to Shorty that same evening, 'Gene Norman would like us to do a record together, how about it?' 'Yeah man, good idea.' And what did Shorty do? He did the record with another tenor player. A white guy. He was afraid that I was too strong for him.

"Dick Bock of Pacific Records heard about the success of the Lighthouse All Stars. Now, I'm the star, right? But he went to the Lighthouse and he hired everybody but me! I could not understand that. I said, 'What's happening, man? I'm the star, every night I have a lot of success, and you hire all the cats but me! It's crazy.'

"I had to play in burlesque houses and strip joints to survive. In trios with percussion and piano, without bass. The whole evening I was allowed to play just the melody. For years, I worked with drummers who couldn't keep time and pianists who played wrong chords. One of the bandleaders was a vibraphonist who couldn't play at all. He was tone deaf. He knew where the notes were, but not how they sounded. If you played him two notes, he couldn't tell you which was higher. I always made fun of him for it. That's what the situation of the black musicians was in California at the time."

Concerning the break-up of Chet and Mulligan, all sorts of stories have been related. One thing is clear: the personalities of the two men were always basically unlike. Mulligan found Chet difficult, and Chet felt the same about him. It is not hard to find the reasons for their incompatibility.

Mulligan was two-and-a-half years older, a professional musician from the age of seventeen. He had to fight for every dollar. Chet, on the other hand, was just out of the army when they met. He was completely inexperienced, and success came to him immediately. Unlike Mulligan, he never studied or practiced hard. Mulligan came from a strict, religious family; Chet was a pampered boy who

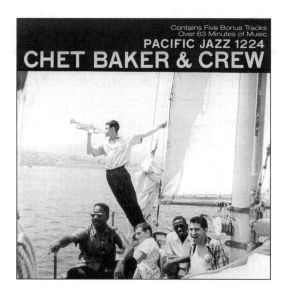

"Chet Baker &
Crew," 1956

hadn't learned to be responsible. Mulligan had come to LA deliberately to advance his career. There he stumbled on Chet. But Chet already showed signs of reckless behavior. While Mulligan was organizing a rehearsal band and was busy composing and arranging, Chet's life, he remembers, was one long party. "He's always have this pack around—Californians, surfer types—and there'd always be five or six of them . . . We'd get done and these guys would drive up to the mountains to ski. By the time they got there the sun was up. They'd ski through the morning then go down to the beach and sail. By then the day's gone by and Chet comes to the gig. He'd do that two, three days in a row, without sleeping, and his chops would dry out; he'd have trouble with chapped lips and he'd start missing notes. I'd say to him, 'Chet, have you ever heard of sleep? It's a wonderful thing for your chops'" (*Down Beat*, January 1989).

Chet's first run-in with the law occurred on December 23rd 1952—that is, on his 23rd birthday—when he was arrested for possession of narcotics. With that his rap sheet begins. 'Narcotics' in this case refers to soft drugs—marijuana, specifically, which, according to his account, he had smoked regularly since junior college (*As though I had wings*, 28, 59).

The penalty, however, for a first offense was limited to a fine and three years' probation. During the next three years, however, Chet would be arrested several times more for drugs, occasionally too for driving drunk. Though no stranger to drugs himself, Mulligan seems to have had little patience with such behavior. Truth to tell, the baritone saxophonist was known for having a rather overbearing personality. And he was not exactly adept—at least yet—in commercial affairs. Bassist Red Mitchell: "When Mulligan wanted to form his own band, I was his first choice. He invited me to auditions. I had no great wish to join because I knew Gerry, we had already played together a lot. We met in Phil Turetsky's house to record a few pieces*, but I soon had enough of it. I told him to ask somebody else. So Gerry went on with different bass players, but he kept calling to invite me for this gig or that. Two years later, in 1954, he showed up with a very attractive offer: a four-week tour of Europe, princely sums of money. I said, 'OK Gerry, you win. But only if I can bring my wife.' So Gerry says, 'I'll take care of it, no problem.' It turned out completely different. First of all,

---

*"Get Happy," "S'Wonderful," and "Godchild"; all on *The Original Gerry Mulligan Quartet with Chet Baker*.

there was suddenly no money left over for my wife's airline ticket and hotel. So she had to stay home. And then, just before we left, the four weeks suddenly turned into one. We had a lot of success, incidentally. The audience at the Salle Pleyel in Paris went nuts. The concert was released on a record that sells well even today. And I have never seen a single penny for it! Recently I even saw it out on CD."

In June 1953, shortly after a recording session for which the quartet was expanded to include Lee Konitz, Mulligan was arrested for drugs. In September, after a long detention, the saxophonist was sentenced to three months in a prison euphemistically entitled The California Honor Farm. Chet went out and hired pianist Russ Freeman, an old friend, as a replacement for their dates at the Haig. Soon after (July) he and Freeman entered the studio together. Chet's group was as successful as Mulligan's. That year, he won both the Critics and the Readers Poll in *Down Beat*. By comparison: in the Readers Poll the previous year he had only placed 21st. In November, Chet played a few weeks again with Parker, on a West Coast tour up to Vancouver.

Mulligan was released from prison after Christmas, cured of his addiction. A few days later Chet ran into him on Hollywood Boulevard. "I said I'd work for [him] again, and that I didn't care what we did—club dates, concerts, whatever—but I wanted three hundred dollars a week" (*As though I had wings*, 63–64). This was twice what he Gerry had earlier paid him. According to Chet, Mulligan laughed in his face. For the time being, at least, that ended any chance there was of reuniting. Friends of

Mulligan tend to interpret this as evidence of Chet's churlishness: A friend gets out of prison, and he leaves him in the lurch. But after winning all the polls, Chet felt he had every right to a raise in salary.

Mulligan left for New York, where he further explored the pianoless concept with Bob Brookmeyer, a serious, technically accomplished young valve-trombonist, whose personality was undoubtedly more suited to his own. Chet and Gerry would reunite in 1957 and 1974,* but long-term collaboration was apparently impossible. Chet in a November 1983 interview with *Jazz Hot*: "That's out of the question. He himself wants nothing more to do with me. He's furious with me! Because I managed to start something without him. And he doesn't want to support it. I would have done well to remain his trumpeter the rest of my life, I think . . . It's stupid, because even if we would stay together only one year for a world tour, it would be fantastic in a financial sense. We would be able to play in the big stadiums, just like the rock groups."

Mulligan is more conciliatory when the subject of his former sideman comes up. In interviews, again and again, he praises Chet's musical abilities. And if the discussion turns personal, he usually says something like, We didn't get along especially well. "It's just that some people you like to hang out with and some people you don't" (*Down Beat*, January 1989). In *Let's Get Lost*, he

*1957: *Reunion: Gerry Mulligan with Chet Baker* (EMI/Manhattan Records CDP 7 46857 2); 1974: *Gerry Mulligan/Chet Baker: Carnegie Hall Concert* (CBS/Epic 4505542)

says: "I believe that Chet is maybe the most gifted trumpeter with whom I ever played or ever heard. There was a direct line from his musical ideas to his trumpet."

Baker's success provoked a heated debate in jazz circles. It developed into an embarrassing controversy about a young white trumpeter, who had gotten rich, while Miles Davis, widely regarded as his model, was being short-changed. Even if the Miles-vogue was only to come later, Chet was already a big admirer of Miles and other black trumpeters of the time, including Dizzy Gillespie. He seemed unaware of the black–white arguments he himself had ignited, and owned up to his influences with naïve sincerity.

Carol Baker: "Chet never thought he was better than Dizzy or Miles. Not then and not later. For him they were trumpeters on a whole different level; he looked up to them. But at the same time he didn't have any inferiority complex. He thought of himself as a decent trumpeter who had a right to a decent salary. In the '70s, he always said to me: 'I play ten times better today than I did then, and I don't show up in a single poll anymore.'"

The following dialogue, excerpted from a record with live material from the mid-'50s,* shows (among other things) Chet's indifference to the supposed opposition between the styles of jazz on either coast. He is being interviewed on the Tonite Show.

Moderator: "You have a very pleasant sound; I think you can get a lot of educated people interested in jazz because you make a very pleasant noise. Let's take

*_Trumpet Geniuses of the Fifties_ (Philology 214 W 13)

With Phil Urso.

© Ray Avery

Dizzy Gillespie. He plays fantastic. But I have noticed that even people who know nothing about jazz can appreciate your sound, you know, they understand what the sounds mean. Dizzy has a . . . sharp, shrill sound. Does his sound disturb you, artistically, or is it all right for him?"

Chet: "Not in the least. Dizzy is a big favorite of mine. Miles also."

Moderator: "Hmmm. Right. Just see, what can I say . . . How old are you, Chet?"

Chet: "Twenty-four."

Moderator: "Twenty-four. When you fatten up . . . " (*Incomprehensible, laughter from the audience*).

Chet: "I've lost ten pounds in the last four months."
Moderator: "Lost ten pounds? On the road? Looking for a new mouthpiece? (*Laughter from the audience.*) Or just on tour?"

Chet: "On our last tour we logged 20,000 miles."

Moderator: "O, how awful. Well as long as you have fun, that's what matters. Tomorrow night you play Birdland, correct?"

Chet: "Tomorrow night."

Moderator: "Who comes after you?"

Chet: "Sarah Vaughan, I believe . . . I'm not exactly sure."

Moderator: "Well, Birdland is the place to go for the best in jazz. And what will you play now?"

Chet: "A composition by Gerry Mulligan, named 'Motel'."

Moderator: "All right, let's hear it."

'a touch of genius':
chet and russ freeman

*a*fter breaking with Mulligan, Chet again hooked up with an experienced musician—Russ Freeman, three-and-a-half years his senior (born May 28, 1926) and an active member since 1945 in the LA jazz scene. The quartet with Freeman lasted (with two brief interruptions) from the end of June 1953 until August 1955. After that, the pair still teamed in the studio occasionally. Freeman plays on both of Chet Baker's two best LPs from the '50s: *Chet Baker Sings* (1954/56), and *Quartet* (1956).

Russ Freeman: "From the start we got on well together. We met the first time at the end of 1951. Chet had just gotten out of the army and was still completely unknown. He lived with his first wife Charlaine in Lynwood. Behind their apartment there was a small, freestanding little house that we used as a practice area. We didn't perform publicly, but we practiced a lot together. At his place, at my place—wherever we could. Already he played just like he did later, more or less. In 1953, after my divorce from my first wife, we lived for a while together: Chet, Charlaine, and I. We had a house in Hollywood Hills. He played with Gerry at that time, I had a job with the Lighthouse All Stars. When we went on tour with the quartet, it was all over between Charlaine and Chet, and we moved out of the house."

Freeman does not believe that Chet was influenced by Miles Davis. "He hardly knew Miles at the beginning. The Miles influence didn't start until later—in 1954, at Birdland. We played there opposite Miles Davis. That was an unlucky combination of circumstances, because Chet had long since found his own style. But he heard Miles playing there every night, and he came under his influence. The influence didn't last very long—five years at most, I think. After that he returned to his own thing. I lost track of him a little later on. But then I've listened to records from the '60s and '70s, and on them I can hear that he found his way back to his own style."

Bud Shank: "You can't simply dismiss Chet as a Miles Davis imitator. Chet Baker was Chet Baker. He was an important figure in history, and he must remain so in memory. He influenced many musicians. In the '50s there were a lot of trumpeters who imitated him in every respect. They stood in the same attitude, they played each note the way he would. He was more imitated than imitator."

Chet has always claimed that he started 'chipping'—i.e., shooting heroin, sometimes cocaine, often the two together—in 1956, after a European tour. So, for instance, in the memoir, he writes, "At that point [1956] I was very naïve about being strung out on stuff" (*As though I had wings*, 69). Freeman, however, remembers it differently. By 1956, he says, Chet was already using regularly. "It started at the end of 1954, at the time we had the quartet together. Chet was incredibly popular already, and played well—I don't understand why he was so irrational. It had nothing to do with stage fright or anything like that. In that respect, he never had to worry. He started to use right around the time everybody else was stopping. Drugs were going out of fashion. I was also strung out for a time, but I had stopped just when we started the quartet in June 1953. Chet was also the only guy who continued so long while other junkies either quit or died. In the '40s and '50s, an awful lot of musicians died because of drugs. Art Pepper was the only other exception; he was addicted a very long time. He finally did manage to quit—but then he died as a result."

In an interview with *Jazz Hot* in 1983, Chet gave his own version of how his dependence started; the story was taken up by the entire jazz press and by other magazines as well. He says he started in 1956 when he returned from Europe. "I got married for a second time, and that was a big mistake. The fact that I was no longer as popular

in the States as I had been before was maybe also a factor."
On top of that, the death of the pianist Dick Twardzik
was supposed to be an additional reason for him to resort
to the needle.

But when Chet started on drugs in 1954, he had not yet
met his second wife, Twardzik was still alive and well,
and Chet himself was still at the height of his fame.

Chet in the same interview about his heroin use: "Now
it's practically over, I think. One of the reasons is that it
has become so much more expensive. If you have to
struggle to make a living with jazz, you don't always have
the money for it. And if you like cocaine, you have to
earn double in order to mix the two. Every day, you have
to find the money again. In the '50s, drugs were much
cheaper, and the quality was better. You could really buy
a good dose of heroin for three dollars."

In the first year of the quartet with Freeman, Chet was
still performing well. His playing sometimes reached an
amazing level. Russ Freeman: "He had a touch of genius.
When he was in form, he played as well as the best musicians I've met—on the same level as Bird, Diz . . . whoever. I played with Charlie Parker once, in Howard
McGhee's band. I was just a beginner, but by luck I got
the chance to play with him. So I know what it's like to
work alongside a genius. And Chet was on the same
level. He could have the same emotional impact. He had
an original approach. He was a thinking artist. His
improvisations were not simply a bunch of licks, they
were small compositions. Sometimes he was in such daz-
zling form that it embarrassed me. He blew a solo, and if

I was to go next, I would think to myself, What is the point of playing another piano solo? He's already said everything there is to say. I could only do a pale repetition.

"In a theoretical sense, Chet was a total illiterate. He never knew what key he played in. He also had nothing to rely on if he happened to be having a bad day. I must admit that Chet was not in form on occasion, especially after he started with the drugs. He could already read a little music in the studio. The parts of course could not be too hard. I cannot remember that he ever wrote anything down in musical notation. That's probably also the reason he never composed anything, so far as I know."

Certainly, Chet was not a prolific composer. But "Freeway"—which he recorded with Mulligan—is credited to him. And he is listed as co-composer of four Italian songs from the year 1962. Most of his other compositional efforts —as for example on *Blues for a Reason*, a record with Warne Marsh from 1984—are in reality improvisations over a chord sequence, to which a title was later appended.

Bud Shank is convinced that Chet's technical proficiency was not that limited. "I recorded some records in the '50s and '60s with him, and I'm sure he read the music as well as the changes. All right, he was no great reader, but he managed. And he must have known something about chords or he never could have played Russ Freeman's pieces. Those are complicated songs, you can't just play them by ear. Chet could also play a little piano. Very slowly and in only a few keys, but still.

"In the '60s, we recorded a number of pop songs: 'Michelle,' 'California Dreamin',' a few more. There were sessions in which you had to read from the sheet music. We only had limited time at our disposal because studio hours are expensive. Chet did this type of work like a real pro. He never gave the impression that he was unsure of himself."

On October 27, 1953 Chet made his first recordings as a singer—the ballads "The Thrill is Gone" and "I Fall in Love Too Easily." Three months later, he made another, better version of the second piece.

Opinions about Chet's singing still vary widely. Jazz critics —especially the critics at the time—had scarcely a kind word for his vocal efforts. Many fans, however, went crazy over his high, pure, vibrato-less voice. Herbie Hancock in *Let's Get Lost*: "He sang romantic ballads in a smooth, smoky voice. Many people would agree that he played a very important part in their love life."

It is not clear who first got the idea of recording Chet as a singer. The producer Dick Bock of Pacific Records claims he made the suggestion after hearing him sing at a club. Chet corroborated this later: "It was his idea . . . I was singing one number a set at the time." Russ Freeman, however, does not remember hearing Chet sing prior to the recording. "The first time I heard Chet sing? That was on the first vocal session for Pacific. He didn't sing on the stage so much, you know. Later, when he had tooth problems, he started to sing more. To be honest, I was never much a fan of his singing. I always found that male as well as female singers got too much attention. Maybe that was prejudice. I didn't like the idea of Chet singing at all. It only distracted from what was going on instrumentally. But of course I did my job. I functioned as Chet's musical director. I picked out the pieces for him, I wrote the arrangements, and I also composed one or two numbers."

Freeman describes the climate in the band as 'real good'. "There were difficulties sometimes of course, but that is inevitable. Here we were, eight of us on the road, four young men and four pretty girls. That easily leads to conflict. It also happens when young people go on vacation together. But we were always able to talk about it. Chet was somebody you got along with easily. He was an easygoing person. He was open to every suggestion. He made few demands. If there were problems, it was usually because of money or a girl. We didn't earn an awful lot if you take into account that we had trip and hotel expenses. There would be some grumbling if we stayed in bad hotels or had to play in funky clubs. Now the working conditions for jazz musicians in California have improved somewhat.

"Toward the end of 1954, when we played Birdland for the third or fourth time, I left the band after a big dust-up with Chet. Chet at that time had a relationship with a French girl who tried to insulate him from the other band members. She pulled us to pieces. I can't remember the details and I also can't remember what her name was. But she was certainly the reason I drove back to LA. Fortunately the conflict was resolved quickly, and by the beginning of 1955 I was back in his quartet.

"I was, I think, the oldest person in the band, and besides being pianist I was musical director and road manager as well. I arranged the transportation, I booked the hotels, and I took care of the finances. A hard job. I wonder today where I got the energy. You simply could not leave anything for Chet to do. He was completely naive. He had no business head and he never had a business head. I'll give you an example. After the incident with the French girl, I gave Chet a part of the salary, which we still had to pay taxes on. Since I was responsible for the finances, the money was in my account. It was approximately 3,000 dollars. I left the band, so I got the money out of the bank and gave it to Chet with the necessary instructions. So now *he* had to take care of it. It was none of my concern. And what did Chet do? He drove to Detroit and bought himself a Jaguar with it. That was Chet. He still had problems with the IRS for years after that. Whatever he had, he spent immediately."

The 'French girl' is probably Lili (or Liliane) whom Chet mentions in the memoir: "In New York, I met a Parisian girl named Liliane. She was just twenty-two, and she traveled with me for the next two years. Charlaine and I had been drifting for some time, and Liliane was like a breath of fresh air. She was quick, beautiful, and played chess well" (*As though I had wings*, 65).

Russ Freeman: "Chet was quite a normal kid, in the sense that he showed up promptly on stage, dressed well, and so on. The real problems only began in the spring of 1955 when I returned to the band. He was now truly addicted. He became unreliable. [Drummer] Bob Neel had disappeared and Chet in the meantime had hired a

Chet and Lili,
September 1955.
© Ed van der Elsken

drummer who was also a junkie, Peter Littman. The boy was exactly twenty years old. An impossible kid. The working relationship was anything but agreeable. The devil only knows what became of [Littman]. [Bassist] Jimmy Bond was clean and he stayed clean. He's been in LA for years now. Jimmy is a successful businessman; a nice fellow. I sometimes run into him and we talk about old times. Shortly before a long European tour, I finally left the group. There were several reasons for it. Chet was addicted, his drummer was addicted, and there is always a division between musicians who are clean and those who are using. Addicts hang with other addicts. Our old friendship no longer existed. I finally had enough of bearing all the responsibility. Chet was the leader officially, but in practical terms I had to take care of everything. I had constant headaches, a kind of migraine. After I left the group, I played for years in the band of [drummer] Shelly Manne. We played night after night in his club, Shelly Manne's Hole. Sometimes I met Chet when he visited the club.

Dick Twardzik.

"My replacement was Dick Twardzik, a young pianist from Boston. I had heard Dick in 1954 when we played with the quartet in Boston. We were all excited by his playing. I immediately called Dick Bock of Pacific Records and said: 'There's a young guy here who plays piano like you wouldn't believe. You have to record him.' Dick Bock agreed right away. He let Twardzik make a record that I produced." Chet in 1983: "'He was a friend of our drummer [Peter Littman], he had just gone through rehab in Lexington [Kentucky] and was clean." Twardzik jammed once with the band, and Chet hired him on the spot.

Russ Freeman: "A year later I left the band and Chet and I were in agreement: Dick Twardzik had to be the new pianist. The thing turned out tragically, I'm sure you know the story. Not two months later, Dick died of an overdose. He was 24.

"In 1956, we did two sessions for *Chet Baker Sings*. After that we played only one time together—on the album *Quartet* from 1956. I believe that to be the best record we did together. The way he plays 'Love Nest' on it . . .

"I spoke with him for the last time about four years before his death. He called me and asked whether I wanted to do a European tour with him. I passed on it. The financial conditions were not very attractive and were not going to get better. Furthermore, I was incredibly busy with studio jobs and arranging. We would have had to arrange a lot before I could leave Los Angeles. In retrospect I regret that I didn't do it . . . Well, things can't be changed now."

In 1983 Chet mentioned a plan of Japanese organizers to reunite him with Freeman and the rhythm section from that period—Carson Smith and Bob Neel. Chet thought it was a great idea, and Wim Wigt was prepared to sponsor the project. But Freeman again declined.

Freeman: "In the last ten years of my career I was a dance arranger. I wrote the music arrangements, sometimes also the compositions, for many big television shows. The Andy Williams Show, the Academy Awards show, variety shows, you name it. It was a terrible job. I hated every minute of it, but it paid well. In 1987, when I could afford it financially, I quit working. Since then I haven't touched the piano. I still sometimes get telephone calls from people asking me whether I want to play this gig or that. I always say, 'Sorry, but I don't play anymore. There are so many good young musicians in LA, just ask them.' 'But why,' they ask, 'don't you have the time?' And I say, 'Because I just don't want to anymore. I worked my whole life, and now I no longer work. It has been beautiful but I'm retired.'

"I played jazz for the last time in 1982. I did a duet album for the Japanese market with Shelly Manne. I've heard little about it since then."

a drama in paris: the
first drug problems

*i*n the years 1953 to 1958, Chet was at the height of his popularity. The summer of 1953 he was awarded the New Star Award in *Down Beat*'s Critics Poll. In 1953 and 1954 he won their Readers Poll, as well as getting top honors in *Metronome* in 1954 and 1956, *Melody Maker* in 1955, *Jazz Echo* in 1956 and 1958, and *Playboy* in 1958. There are today, more than thirty years later, still many fans who go into raptures when Chet's music from this era is discussed. "He was the Boy Next Door, the sound of introspection on a summer evening fire escape, the sonority successor to Bix . . . His melancholy tone and simple lyricism seemed to linger in the nerve endings long after the last notes had sounded . . . And his voice cast the same forlorn, little-boy-lost shadow, causing co-eds to swoon clean out of their saddle Oxfords."*

The Dutch author Jules Deelder first heard Chet in 1954, on the occasion of his older sister's birthday. He was nine years old: "I found it a strange music; I had just grown used to the Dutch Swing College Band, but this was completely different. Chet's voice gave me goosebumps. I had never heard such a voice! So distant and so

*Roy Carr, Brian Case, and Fred Dellar, *The Hip* (London 1986), 78–80

close at the same time . . . It sounded so . . . forlorn. I didn't know how to describe it. I left the room with a kink in my neck. For hours more I sat at the landing, motionless, listening until my parents came home. I could not sleep that night. I hovered between dreaming and awake and heard Chet Baker haunt through my head and over the stairway."*

At the beginning of 1955, Chet played a small role in Tom Gries' war film *Hell's Horizon*. The film deals with a military unit that has been assigned to carry out a bombing mission in Korea—an unexceptional film, which was coolly received by the critics. The film could have been the start of a real film career, however. Bud Shank: "When I met Chet, he was poised to become a film star. Everyone was certain of it. He was no experienced actor of course, but he had a certain presence. Chet was a good-looking kid, and he could sing and play. He could have done something with it if he had not gotten involved with the chemicals. The question is whether he would have wanted such a career. A movie star's life is frightful."

There is a photo of Chet from July 1954. He is leaning against something, surrounded backstage by some pic-ture-pretty, but rather square-looking girls. They wear the wide, pleated 'poodle' skirts fashionable at the time. He is seen chatting casually with them: Chet as charis-matic star, the newest Frank Sinatra.[†] Chet in *Jazz Hot*

---

*Jules Deelder, *Modern Passé* (Amsterdam 1984)

[†]The photo can be found in the booklet included with *The Complete Pacific Jazz Live Chet Baker/Russ Freeman* (Mosaic MD3-113); and in *Young Chet*, p. 63.

(November 1983): "I soon became aware that that there wasn't enough time or opportunity to kiss all the girls in the world. The best thing is to stay cool—just be choosy and wait for the right opportunity."

On September 6, 1955, Chet traveled to Europe with his new group—pianist Dick Twardzik, bassist Jimmy Bond and drummer Peter Littman. The tour was originally to last four months, but was extended to eight. Chet played all over Europe, from the Keflavik Air Base in Iceland to southern Italy. His relationship with Lili, his French girl-friend, had something to do with his visit. "I had an affair with a girl from Paris who had to return to France, so I decided to follow her. And I wanted to see Europe" (*Jazz Hot*, November 1983). Factors that would eventually motivate Chet to make a life for himself in Europe were also in play already: the enthusiasm of the European jazz fans, the slower pace of life—even if this tour was hard-ly a rest-cure—and easier access to drugs.

On September 17 Chet appeared in the Amsterdam Concertgebouw. The author Remco Campert was among the many Dutch fans who saw Chet perform live for the first time at this concert. "His fame had preceded him, and the hall was sold out. When he played—the slight musician who looked like an American GI—it was dead quiet; you could hear a pin drop. When he sang 'My Funny Valentine,' everyone in the room had a lump in the throat. Beautiful moments."*

Jazzjaarboek 4 (Amsterdam 1985)

On September 23, Chet was offered a contract by the French label Barclay for no fewer than seven LPs. Some tragic things took place in the course of the tour however, and in the end Chet would only record music enough for a little over three. The first session was nearly all devoted to the compositions of Bob Zieff, a friend of Dick Twardzik's from Boston. They are dreamy pieces with unconventional harmonies and melodies.

Twardzik's piano playing is hard to categorize. He doesn't play like Bud Powell, or Monk—basically not like any of the well-known pianists of the time. The pianist himself said that he was inspired by classical composers like Berg and Schönberg. Chet in *Let's Get Lost*: "The first time I heard him play, I couldn't believe it. He had somehow bridged the thing between classical and jazz. He played so well, and I didn't even know that he was using anything until a concert in Switzerland somewhere, in Zurich I think. He passed out backstage one night and a doctor who was in the audience came in, and that was how I found out what was going on. He had been getting high for several months at that point, and he died about a month later. The day after we made an album they found him in his hotel room. I would say he was one of the four best piano players I ever had a chance to play with."

Here, Chet's memory fails him somewhat. Twardzik died not one but ten days after the session. On September 21, 1955 he died of an overdose in his Parisian hotel room in the Rue St. Benoit. Chet: "I was totally clean. Dick's overdose made me feel horrible. His family thought I was responsible although I had no idea about the whole

With Halema backstage at the Armory, Rochester NY, 1956.

© Paul J. Hoeffler

situation" (*Jazz Hot*, November 1983). Chet indeed can hardly be blamed for Twardzik's drug use. But he may have devised the story that he was clean at the time to avoid any suggestion of involvement in his death.

Two days after this calamity, Chet was scheduled to appear in London. Owing to the regulations of the local Musicians Union he was not permitted to play trumpet. Instead, accompanied by the French pianist Raymond Fol, he sang four standards, before his feelings overwhelmed him and forced him to terminate the concert. The atmosphere in the group had not been good, and Twardzik's death did nothing to bring the musicians together. Immediately after the London concert a vehement

67

dispute arose between Chet and Littman, and the drummer promptly departed for the States. The Swede Nils-Bert Dahlander has to substitute at the recording date planned for the following day. Dahlander is soon gone himself, and in November Jimmy Bond leaves also. It is almost as if a curse lies on Chet's groups: bassists, pianists, drummers, even saxophonists constantly come and go. Chet now has to manage the band himself, and he doesn't manage all too well.

The live recording of this European tour sounds uninspired.* Chet was suffering from tooth decay in this period, and because he was already handicapped by the absence of his front tooth, it bothered him that much more. In the studio, with a producer, arrangements and a time limit, Chet sounds more assured. Parts of the last session with Twardzik, together with the session that took place three days after Twardzik's death, were released on the LP *Chet Baker in Europe / A Jazz Tour of the NATO Countries* (Pacific Jazz PJ 1218).

On April 4, 1956, Chet returned to the United States. His romance with Lili had run its course, and he got married now for the second time. Again, it was to be a brief marriage. Carol Baker: "Chet's second wife was named Halema [pronounced Ha-LEE-ma; maiden name, Halema Ali]. She came from Detroit and saw him playing there in a club. They got married right away, because he could not have taken her on tour otherwise. They had known each other exactly six weeks! It quickly became

---

The Great Lars Gullin Vol. 1 (Dragon DRCD 224) and *Live in Europe* (Accord 139229)

clear that they were not compatible. It was a rash decision to marry so fast. It was no one's fault. With Halema, Chet had his first child: Chesney. Chet Junior was born in San Francisco in 1957. He has the same name, but was called Chesney to distinguish him from his father."

According to some sources, Chet and Halema were actually acquainted before that. In the memoir he says they married not six weeks but 'about six months' after they met (*As though I had wings*, 72). And the results of a photo session with the couple by William Claxton are labeled 'Helima [sic] and Chet Baker, Redondo Beach, California, 1955' (*Young Chet*, 80–84). The date is problematic in that Chet and Lili were still together in 1955.

However that may be, the Halema in the photos is a distinguished-looking, reserved woman with dark hair and manicured hands. She was of Pakistani–East Indian origin. As early as July 31, 1956, not four months after his return from Europe, Chet and his tenor player Phil Urso recorded a piece composed by Urso entitled 'Halema.' When Halema had to appear with Chet before an Italian court (for dope smuggling) in 1961, the pair were still married. Carol: "I met Halema in Italy. After that I pretty much lost track of her for years, until Chet's burial. After the burial, she called me a few times. I think she is a very nice lady."

Later, Halema re-married and moved to Los Angeles, where she continues to reside. She was at Chet's burial, but kept herself in the background. According to Peter Huijts, she seemed barely involved in the ceremony on an emotional level. Their son, Chesney, did not attend.

Halema took no part in the production of *Let's Get Lost*; unlike Carol and Chet's later girlfriends Ruth Young and Diane Vavra, she doesn't appear in the film personally. She doesn't seem to want to have anything to do with the Chet Baker industry. While Carol Baker later constantly stood for interviews with the press and adorned the covers of magazines, Halema has always held aloof from public attention. (Her name is often incorrectly reported as Helima or Halima.)

In 1956, however, things were still going well for Chet. He was appearing regularly in concert and in the studio. With Phil Urso and the pianist Bobby Timmons he established a quintet rounded out with Jimmy Bond and Peter Littman (Chet appears to have settled his differences with the drummer). It is apparent now that he intends to play more powerful, bop-oriented music. Robert Gordon dismisses Chet's vocal recordings out of hand in his book *Jazz West Coast*, while enthusiastically praising the neo-bop group with Urso [Robert Gordon, *Jazz West Coast* (London and New York, 1986)]. In this respect, he is merely repeating the opinion of most critics at the time. According to the reviewers, Chet has found his way to real jazz. The new approach can be heard on a series of recordings with this quintet and on the aforementioned album *Quartet* with Russ Freeman (Pacific Jazz PJ 1232). Chet managed to win over even the most grudging critics with his dynamic playing here—amazingly, because he had to contend with sore teeth again on the date. The most praised number from this session, 'Love Nest,' was produced only after great effort. Chet already had a few unsatisfactory takes behind him when the producer, Woody Woodard, suggested trying it again on mute. Chet is reluctant at first, but makes the attempt and this time blows a brilliant solo. In October 1956 the music was recorded for *Playboys* with Urso and alto saxophonist Art Pepper. Most of the compositions and arrangements were written by Jimmy Heath.*

Heath: "*Playboys* was an authentic junkie record. Art Pepper was just out of jail, Chet was arrested a week after the session, and piano player Carl Perkins would die two years later. When the record was recorded I was behind bars myself. In 1955 I was caught with narcotics and had to serve almost five years. Luckily I was allowed to keep my saxophone in the cell, and I composed a lot during the time. They had to come fetch the music for *Playboys* from jail."

Two days after recording the soundtrack for *The James Dean Story* on November 8, 1956, Chet was arrested for the first time for possession of hard drugs. He is sentenced to a two-month stay in Federal Hospital in Lexington, Kentucky.

In February 1957, he makes an American tour with the Birdland All Stars, and later that year tours Italy and Sweden with his own group. Oddly enough, no recordings are made during this second European tour. Only in August 1957, after returning to Los Angeles, would Chet go back into the studio again, this time as part of an impromptu big band under the leadership of Jack Sheldon.† Then he resettled in New York. Here he ran

---

*Pacific Jazz PJ 1234; reissued on EMI/Pacific Jazz P 32-5351

†*Jack Sheldon and his All Star Band* (Crescendo/GNP GNPS 9036)

into Mulligan, who was doing arrangements for a series of records with Dick Bock. This series features a reunion between him and Chet, as well as a recording on which the two accompany the singer Annie Ross.* These records are only intermittently successful. Chet has since outgrown the pianoless approach and is audibly pressed to adapt himself. It's like listening to a Gerry Mulligan quartet in which Chet Baker has accidentally replaced Art Farmer, say, or Jon Eardley. Chet and Mulligan have apparently patched things up, because the saxophonist also secured for Chet a recording date with Verve: *Stan Meets Chet*. This record was out of print for years—understandably. Both he and Getz sound weary and uninspired.[†] Later in the same year Bill Grauer of the Riverside label, based in New York, invited Chet to record for him. Although they never had a formal contract (owing in part to Chet's erratic habits), Chet would make five records for Riverside, all stylistically and qualitatively very different from each other. They include a successor to *Chet Baker Sings*, and a compelling hard bop session with Johnny Griffin.[††]

In February 1959, Chet is arrested in New York for possession. He is sentenced to six months on Riker's Island, and suffers through withdrawal in his frigid cell. On top of that, he loses his cabaret card, which means that for the time being he cannot perform live in New York. He

---

Reunion (EMI / Manhattan / Pacific Jazz CDP 7 468572; *Annie Ross Sings a Song with Mulligan* (EMI / Manhattan / Pacific Jazz CDP 7 468522)

[†]Verve MGV 8263, reissued by MGM

[††]*It Could Happen to You: Chet Baker Sings* (OJC CD 303-2); *Chet Baker in New York* (OJC CD 207-2)

is released after four months (good behavior), then makes his last record for Riverside, *Chet Baker Plays the Best of Lerner and Loewe* (OJC 137). His playing here is flat and unfocused. If he is caught with drugs again, a sentence of several years is inevitable. And so Chet takes the money he's earned from Riverside and immediately heads to Europe with Halema and Chesney in tow. In August, he plays with Kenny Clarke and René Urtreger in the Parisian Blue Note, then works in Italy. His relationship with Riverside, never formalized to begin with, is now effectively over.

the second european
tour: a picaresque
journey through
clinics and jails

*C*het was received warmly in Italy. He formed a group with local musicians and couldn't complain about lack of work. Another album 'with strings' follows, and the film composer Piero Umiliani liked to make use of his services.*

While in Europe Chet renewed his friendship with Jacques Pelzer. He had already met the Belgian saxophonist and flutist on his first visit to Europe. Chet would remain friends with him longer than with just about anyone else; up to his death, Pelzer's house in Belgium remained a place of refuge. Pelzer gave him a roof over his head, looked after Chet's young family when Chet had to do jail time in Italy, and played hundreds of concerts with him—often unpaid.

In his day job, Pelzer was a pharmacist. Initially, he tended the drugstore himself; later he put someone else behind the counter, and finally, shortly before his death,

---

*Chet Baker with Fifty Italian Strings, also under the title *Angel Eyes* (Jazzland/ Victor VDJ-1615; reissued by Fantasy as OJCCD-492-2); *Italian Movies* (Liuti Records LRS 0063)

he gave up the store altogether. Pelzer, five years older than Chet, was living with his second wife in a house in the Belgian town of Luik furnished in Early Bohemian when I spoke with him in 1989. His record collection dated from the 1950s, his furniture probably earlier than that. The only objects of value were Pelzer's instruments. Interviewing him was extremely difficult. It was hard to clarify for him what the purpose of my visit was. Pelzer spoke a mixture of French and English with now and then a scrap of Flemish thrown in.

Jacques Pelzer: "I 'ave 'ad many musicians live with me 'ere: Dexter Gordon, Archie Shepp, Don Byas, Kenny Clarke, Bud Powell . . . and of all these guys, Chet was the most hip. That's why I'll never move out of here. I will die in this house. So many musical vibrations are 'ere. Chet played in this corner, Stan Getz played there, beside the piano. I still see them all before me. There, on the wall, you see a letter from Sonny Rollins. Thanks to Chet, I've met them all. He gave me my chance to come out. At the beginning of the '50s, Chet's records with Russ Freeman and Gerry Mulligan had already thrilled me. I bought all those 45s. When Chet was in Paris in 1955 I met him there. He was the most beautiful guy in the world. He came to my home, I drove to Paris, and so we got to know each other well. He invited me to Le Chat Qui Pêche in Paris. It was heavenly. He played there with Dick Twardzik, Joe Benjamin [Pelzer probably means Jimmy Bond], and Peter Littman. Chet liked Europe. He had already been here once with an Army band when he was still quite young—he was sixteen or seventeen—shortly after the liberation. We stayed together 33 years, except for the period after 1968, when

Jacques Pelzer in the doorway of his pharmacy.

© Jacky Lepage

he stopped playing. I've met Halema—a nice woman of Pakistani and Indian origin—and Chesney. That was 1959. But I've really got to know Carol Baker. We've spent a lot of time together. I often saw her when Chet was on tour."

Carol Baker was born in 1940 in the English county of Surrey. She met Chet in 1960 and married him in the US in 1965. Carol Baker: "My maiden name is Jackson. In 1960, I went to Italy in search of work. I got a job there with the Shirley Bassey show. It was my task to announce the different performers, in three different languages. I don't speak all those languages, but I had memorized the words. I wore glamorous dresses, a different one for each announcement."

In *Let's Get Lost,* there is a photo of Carol in one of these costumes: a pseudo-Oriental get-up, fashioned from a bikini with all sorts of costume jewelry, high-heeled shoes, a veil, and a gem in her navel.

Carol Baker: "I met Chet in a club. He had just been released from a clinic in Milan where they had done a kind of sleep cure with him. He was completely clean. Later in this year, he started to take something again, but at first quite sporadically and only with a prescription. He kept it hidden from me—I noticed it only after a few months. He had no marks on him."

Carol Baker in Italy, 1961, at time of Chet's release.
© Cecco Maino

The sleep cure was Chet's idea; by this time he was addicted to Jetrium, a German product available without a prescription, and "the closest thing to stuff that I'd ever found." "I was in bad shape—chalky-colored, not eating, and having terrible, frequent chills" (*As though I had wings*, 85). The drug he started to take later in the year was Palfium, another synthetic painkiller available over the counter, in tablets that Chet would dissove and inject.

The trumpeter became a noted figure on the Italian scene at the time. The stories that circulate about him are legion. When he was released from the clinic, he was so eager to get going again that he played in a club for free all night long. The club owner had no more money, and the drummer and the pianist had canceled. Chet and the bass player, Franco Cerri, performed the whole evening as a duet. "At the end of the concert, he embraced me," Cerri told the magazine *Musica Jazz* (July 1988). In Bologna Chet met the pianist Amadeo Tommasi, who had come to the city to play in a local club with a few local musicians. At that time, Italy did not yet have many capable jazz players. Tommasi was on hand for a rehearsal with an apparently very humble band. Chet has no music with him, the musicians speak no English, and no one seems to understand what he wants. The Bolognese musicians gradually become aware of their ignorance, and the situation grows increasingly awkward. Chet keeps cool and asks the pianist of the group whether he can play a particular piece in a different key. The pianist can't do it, so Chet takes the opportunity to replace him with Tommasi. Now things go a whole lot better. Chet asks in broken Italian, "You doing anything tonight? Nothing? You play with me!" (*Musica Jazz*, July 1988).

Chet plays regularly with Romano Mussolini, a fine pianist, but also son of the notorious dictator. After a successful first appearance, he is informed by a colleague about Romano's background. Chet is shocked, but recovers and goes over to the pianist. He puts his hand on his shoulder and says feelingly: "I'm sorry about your old man."

Jacques Pelzer: "In 1960 Chet played with the first edition of the now well-known Comblain festival. He was there with Kenny Clarke. We did a jam session together, and afterward he asked me, 'Would you like to come to Italy with me, Jack?' At that time I didn't know whether anything was going on with jazz there or not. But Chet said, 'There's a good piano player there.' So I said OK. And I jumped in there. But I had bad luck. Chet was arrested on the very day I arrived. I played with his band while he was in prison."

The arrest took place in the summer of 1960. The incident was widely covered in the Italian press. Chet had checked into a clinic in Lucca to deal with his Palfium habit. His doctor, one Lippi Francesconi, would personally drive him to La Bussola di Focetto, a club in neighboring Viareggio, to perform with Romano Mussolini. On July 31, however, the doctor was busy, and allowed Chet to drive to Viareggio alone. Before he takes to the highway in his rented Fiat, Chet decides to take his prescribed injection in the restroom of a gas station near San

Concordia Contrado. It costs him some effort to make
the hit, because his veins are collapsing. After 35 minutes, someone bangs on the door: it's the police. Chet
has to accompany them to the station. There, he tells
them that he has only taken what his doctor has prescribed. Dr. Francesconi is called in to confirm the story,

and a quarter of an hour later Chet is released. According to the newspapers, however, the police had to break the door down, and they found Chet lying on the ground, unconscious, bleeding from several wounds, etc.

Chet in custody.
© Cecco Maino

The sensationalistic press coverage leads to an investigation. A young district attorney questions all the pharmacists in Lucca, and examines all the Palfium scripts. The result is that Chet is charged with illegal possession, smuggling, and theft and forgery of prescriptions. In October, Halema is charged with complicity in Chet's crimes. She has smuggled in eight hundred—according to Chet, four hundred—Palfium tablets from Germany. Chet declares before the court that Halema has brought the pills for him without knowing what the bottles contained. He has been to doctors, he says, who prescribed the drug for his 'terrible headaches.'

Jules Deelder in *Modern Passé* writes: "He was hardly out of prison before he was in the next one. But that didn't prevent word getting out that you could get Palfium pills in Germany without a prescription. The message spread like a wildfire through the European jazz community. From Strasbourg out regular raids on Germany were launched. In two days they went to as many drugstores as they could, then returned to France with pots of pills, where it was a non-stop party until the supply ran out."

Five other accomplices, including Dr. Francesconi, were charged with helping Chet get narcotics. On April 14, 1961 Chet was sentenced to seven years in prison, and Halema—who is identified by two doctors and a lawyer as an accessory—to two years. In September 1961, however, Chet's penalty was reduced in the appellate procedure from seven years to 16 months—which meant that he would be free at the end of December. His lawyer explained to the court that Chet has cured himself of his addiction during his detainment, and, what's more, had composed twenty-two songs in his idle hours.

Chet had indeed written a few compositions—the four, anyway, that he plays on record with the orchestra of Ennio Morricone after his release.* It is the only recordings on which he sings Italian, incidentally. We hear nothing more about the other putative compositions.

*Chet Baker with Ennio Morricone and his Orchestra (RCA, 1962)

Jacques Pelzer: "It was so unjust, to punish such a man. It was unfair. After what he had given the world. Chet never did harm to anybody. I know this man very deeply."

Carol Baker: "I am convinced that the police and the judges were influenced by the sensational reports in the press. The only thing the press were interested in was drugs, drugs, drugs. In every newspaper you ran across, Chet was always associated with drugs. Nothing about his music, only drugs. They never allowed him to get away from that. Nobody was interested when he said that he just wanted to get free of it. Nobody believed it, anyway. They published photos in the Italian papers showing Chet listening to a piano solo with his eyes closed. Now, you know how Chet was when he made music. He concentrated completely. And the photos had a caption like, Just look how stoned he is again. When the photo was made—I was with him, you know—he was as clean as you or me! He was just listening to the piano solo.

"Such experiences depressed Chet. And so he started to think: if you want me to keep being a junkie, then I'll do just that. The press would have had to write: Chet is a great artist, and it is a shame that he is ruining his career. But they didn't write that. The journalists didn't have the least respect for him. Chet was a very gentle and sensitive person. He was a victim of the press and the jazz scene. They did him in."

Not only the gossip sheets, but now the jazz critics turned on him and slammed him with negative notices. John S. Wilson in *The Collector's Jazz* is representative:

"Most of his playing is so vaporous that it seems to be drifting aimlessly in a void . . . The worst, however, is yet to come. For Baker also sings in a flat, dead voice that is even more despondently formless than his trumpet work. The incredible evidence can be found on *Chet Baker Sings*." Only Alun Morgan in *Jazz Monthly* had a more sober assessment (which many critics have since come to support): "Perhaps the root cause of Baker's troubles was early success . . . Within a few years the public (and the critics) that had hailed Baker so readily were quite prepared to drop him from favor and I suspect that he found it impossible to make two readjustments to his status in so short a time" (*Jazz Monthly*, June 1963).

Chet, it seems, was not good for much anymore—either as a person, or as a musician. Jules Deelder writes: "In any event, Chet Baker was through. He cut a deadly trail through Europe, leaving bodies behind left and right, addicted souls who wouldn't hesitate to do their own mother in to come by the coveted stuff—that, at least, was the judgement of the tabloid press. Chet Baker was an unprincipled, broken, degenerate musician spoiled by too much praise, who played trumpet less and less, and sang like a woman instead. A bad example for youth . . . I don't know if it was the result of an organized boycott, but around 1961 you couldn't find a single record by Chet Baker in the stores any more."

While Chet served his time in Lucca, a film company from Rome showed up that wanted to make a movie about his life. The project was canceled, however, when the seven-year sentence came down. The producer was supposed to be Dino de Laurentiis. In 1960, the

American director Michael Anderson had had a similar idea: a drama about a tragic, but oh-so-talented trumpeter, and his various *amours*. The result was *All The Fine Young Cannibals*, a cliché-ridden melodrama starring Robert Wagner as Chad Bixby (~Chet Baker), and Natalie Wood.

After Chet's release on probation in December 1961, photos appear in which he is seen in the company of his new girlfriend, Carol Jackson. At the time of his arrest his marriage to Halema was already strained. This seemed to be the breaking point. Halema herself, according to Carol, was never convicted and was released after being detained six months. She returned to the US and their son, Chesney, who, according to Carol, had been looked after in the meantime by Halema's mother. Halema filed for divorce and married a rich man soon thereafter.

Some days after his release, Chet journeyed to Rome. The director Alberto Lattuada—like Dino de Laurentiis, an important figure in the neo-realist movement—also had plans to make a film of Chet's adventures. The film was never made, but the visit to Rome at least resulted in a memorable album. On January 4, 1962 *Chet is Back* was recorded with the Belgians Bobby Jaspar and René Thomas—undoubtedly Chet's best effort between 1959 and 1973.*

Chet had a good friend in Milan, Nando Latanzzi, who owned the Club Olympia and wanted to help him get

*Now on CD as *The Italian Sessions* (BMG /RCA Victor)

back on his feet. He set aside a small area of the club for him, and hired a bartender and a waiter. The marquis over the separate entrance read: 'The Chet Baker Club.' Chet later described the place to *Down Beat*: "It was very elegant—plush, upholstered chairs, wall-to-wall carpeting, columns in the middle of the room, beautiful little bandstand, velvet drapes on the walls. The lighting was beautiful, and it seated about 80 people comfortably" (*Down Beat*, July 30, 1964).

In April or May 1962, Chet drives to Germany for concerts in Munich and, a broadcast on North German Radio. He is arrested there and has to spend three weeks in the Haar Psychiatric Clinic in Munich. He had stolen prescription forms from a doctor in Munich to get morphine. His drummer, the 37-year-old Donald Scott Brown, is also nabbed for narcotics. After their release, Brown and Chet are barred for two years from entering Germany. Carol gets him out of the sanatorium on June 27, 1962. In a contemporary photo, Chet is seen walking in front, wearing sunglasses, a little dazed to be out in the world again after his latest confinement, carrying some clothes over his arm. Carol follows behind, in a stylish white suit and high heels. She carries Chet's meager possessions in a cardboard box. Although she is pregnant by this time, she seems very thin—thinner, in fact, than she appears in earlier photos. "I'm not leaving him," she tells the press. "When he gets out of the clinic, we intend to go to Switzerland together."

But their plan remains unrealized. In Switzerland, they are *personae non gratae*. Entry to Italy is also refused them. Chet therefore can't get hold of the money that is in an account there, and he loses his contract for two records with RCA. The couple doubles back to Paris, where Chet plays a few weeks in the Blue Note. In August 1962, he travels to London, to participate in the film *Stolen Hours*. He also has hopes that drugs will be easier to get there. They are, thanks to the good offices of an elderly lady doctor named Isabella Frankau. Lady Frankau "was about 75 years old . . . and very businesslike. She simply asked my name, my address, and how much cocaine and heroin I wanted per day" (*As though I had wings*, 97). Dr. Frankau was one of only ten doctors in England licensed to minister to junkies, but in the days before methadone this meant simply supplying their habit. The scripts were cheap—about three-and-a-half dollars each. And Lady Frankau wasn't particular about weaning her patients off the stuff. "After the first day my scripts were all for twenty grams of each, and I was off and running."

Chet played a small supporting role in *Stolen Hours* and recorded a part of the soundtrack. In the autumn, while he is in England, Carol gave birth to their son Dean in Italy. After completion of the film, Chet wanted to remain longer in England (among other things) in order to become a member of their Musicians Union after the mandatory one-year residency period.

But in February 1963, he is arrested again for illegal possession of cocaine. He is held for a while, then on March 27 is deported to France. He works in Paris for eight straight months, with, among others, the Turkish French-horn player Melih Gurel, in the Le Chat Qui Pêche. Pelzer also visits and plays with him.

Jacques Pelzer: "At that time I hadn't played in six months. My first wife had died. That was the only period in my life I went without touching an instrument. Afterward I took my alto and drove to the Adolphe Sax Festival in Dilante. Bobby Jaspar played there with Chet and René Thomas. Chet gave me the courage to continue and invited me to stay in the band. I joined the group for a tour a France. We had a program with Dalida in the first half."

Chet's odyssey takes him to Barcelona, where he completes a month-long engagement in the Club Jamboree with a 'pitiful rhythm section.' "Kenny Drew had been there just before me, and he had walked out on the job and told them they shouldn't even be playing. He gave them a terrible complex, so when I got there they were really scared to death" (*Down Beat* July 30, 1964). It is remarkable that Chet managed to endure an entire month with them as accompanists. The fact that he had found another doctor to write Palfium prescriptions for him helped to make the experience tolerable.

He returns to Paris briefly, then gets an engagement at the Blue Note Club in Berlin. The very first evening there he is arrested and must spend four days in a clinic in Wittenau. Since Chet has been declared 'unstable,' he is spared a prison term. Carol stays with Dean in Berlin and tries to make a living as a babysitter. According to a report in the Dutch magazine *Televizier*, Chet was supposed to give a concert in the Berlin Sport Palace. "Some guards from the clinic were assigned to accompany him and never let him out of their sight . . . [Carol] hopes that one day he will be free of his addiction and then will marry her." After his release, Chet is deported for the

"Chet Baker Arrested!" From BILD-Zeitung, January 23, 1964.

fifth time, this time back to the United States. On March 3, 1964 Chet, Carol, and Dean (then a year old) return to America.

Jacques Pelzer: "When Chet was arrested in Italy in 1960, Carol lived here with me in Luik, Belgium, for a long time. Then she went back to Italy to visit him. After the imprisonment, she tried to join him on his trips, but that was not for her. She came back again here; that caused problems between them. You know, Chet is a pure artist. No one could come between him and the music. I've looked after Dean. When he cried I took him in my arms. Now that he's grown up, I recognize the young Chet in him. He has exactly the same speaking voice, the same appearance.

With Carol, son Dean, and Jacques Pelzer. From BILD-Zeitung, February 1, 1964.

"Chet was so crazy about music. When we traveled in Italy from one place to another, during the day, his thoughts were always on music. He sang instead of telling jokes. He would say, 'Do you know that song? OK, we'll sing it together. You, Jack, sing the melody, the bassist sings the second voice, and I'll sing the third.' That's how we sang in the car. When he stayed here, he would often put a record on and play the bass line on the piano. Many times we jammed, with any guy passing through. Chet was open to everyone who showed up in this provincial backwater.

"Chet was the only man who could put together—as we say in French—*la force et la tendresse*. Strength and tenderness. The combination made him unique. It was the quickest way to make everybody around him happy. So generous at heart. He forced you to listen to other musicians. His concerts were never routine. What he played was pure emotion. And if you start by the feeling, you can't start bad, you know. Because you give the best of yourself. It has nothing to do with how brilliant or how fast you play. He could be the fastest trumpeter in the world! His music was never noisy or disturbing.

"He felt here like it was his home, you know. He had his own room, he could do what he wanted. In his last fifteen years, the poor fellow never had a home. Can you imagine that, such an artist? A year before his death, I had a car accident, and one side of my head was injured. Since then I'm deaf in one hear and have problems with my embouchure. I wondered whether I would ever be able to play again. Chet bucked me up. He said, 'I know you can make it, Jack. You are strong'."

Chet, Jean-Louis Rassinfosse and Jacques Pelzer.

© Jacky Lepage

Bass player Harry Emmery: "Chet needed Pelzer badly of course because of the drugs. But one should not underestimate Pelzer. He could play very beautifully in the style of Paul Desmond. I know very well that Chet was charmed by the way Pelzer played. The man had a sacred respect for Chet, he put in enormous effort for him."

Pelzer is the only European musician who regularly performed with Chet in America. In 1976, the two played twice weekly for some time in New York's Stryker's Bar. They also gave concerts in Chicago, California, Pittsburgh, and Detroit. Pelzer is the father of drummer Micheline Pelzer, who lived some years with the pianist Michel Graillier.

Jacques Pelzer—Chet always called him Jack—died in 1994. Peter Huijts, later Chet's tour manager: "Pelzer was a good fellow. A very dear man. He always took care of Chet. His house in Luik was the only place of refuge for Chet in Europe for years. That friendship cost Pelzer a ton of money."

five toughs from
san francisco:
rock bottom

*W*hile Chet toured the European continent with the police on his heels, the American journalist Jack McKinney wrote an article for *Metronome* in which he quite naturally assumed that Chet was dead [reported in his liner notes to *Groovin'* (Prestige 7460)]. His return to the States, then, attracted some real—if passing—attention. His first appearance back took place in the Cork 'n' Bib in Westbury, Long Island. He had switched to the flugelhorn in the meantime. A French friend had given him the instrument, supposedly after his own trumpet was stolen from Le Chat Qui Pêche in 1963. (A different trumpet had supposedly been stolen earlier, in 1959, during a concert in Naples.) In the Cork 'n' Bib Chet appeared with a borrowed instrument and a mouthpiece with different dimensions than he was used to. According to him, his own flugelhorn was being repaired. That, of course, is possible, but it is a bit strange that he didn't even have his own mouthpiece with him. However that may be, at least one reviewer, Ira Gitler of *Down Beat*, was favorably impressed by what he heard:

"Actually, Baker needed few excuses for his playing, borrowed horn or not. His retention of his lyricism, the addition of greater strength, and his continuance as a stylist mark him as someone to hear at greater length, preferably with his own group" (*Down Beat*, May 21, 1964).

In an interview with Gitler a couple of months later Chet grouses a bit about the flugelhorn: "It's so hard to play, you wouldn't believe it . . . The mouthpiece is deeper and wider, and it takes so much air to fill out this horn . . . If you're not playing steadily, you can't make it."* From this we can perhaps infer that he wasn't, in fact, playing steadily, being preoccupied with other things. Maybe, too, he could conceal his embouchure problems better with the flugelhorn; the instrument is occasionally resorted to by horn players as they get older.

When Chet is interviewed by *Down Beat* that summer, it appears that he is aware of few of the recent innovations on the American scene. Ornette Coleman he has not heard yet. Charles Mingus he has seen, at the Five Spot, but: "I went down there and wasn't impressed at all by what was happening. On the ensembles the things were ragged . . . And Mingus was continually saying things and screaming at different personnel in the band." He has reservations about Coltrane too: "Forty-five minutes is a long time to be blowing; a lot of people get bugged. I'd rather listen to Stan Getz or Al Cohn." But, he adds, "I have heard him play some things that are really beautiful."†

*Down Beat, July 30, 1964
† *Ibid.*

Chet in Boston, 1966 with flugelhorn.
© Lee Tanner

Chet lived in New York for a while with the composer and pianist Tadd Dameron, who was in similar circumstances: little public interest in him, little money, long-term battles with drugs. A potential gig in the Village Vanguard foundered because Chet still could not get the requisite cabaret card. In late 1964 he formed a group with Phil Urso and the pianist Hal Galper (sometimes also Kenny Lowe). With these musicians, he toured the country and made two records for small labels. On both albums, one cannot fail to hear the difficulties he was having with the flugelhorn. On one of them, *Chet Baker Plays and Sings* he performs no fewer than five Dameron compositions—"Mating Call," "Soultrane," "Gnid," "Tadd's Delight," and "Whatever Possessed Me" (Jazz Junction JJ-205). This was probably Chet's way of repaying him for putting a roof over his head. Dameron didn't have long to enjoy the benefits; he died nine months later after a life full of personal problems.

In the summer of 1965 a successful album with Billie Holiday songs is released, on which Chet is accompanied by some studio musicians including Hank Jones and Richard Davis. He has now been under contract with Richard Carpenter for approximately a year. Dameron also worked in his last years for Carpenter; he had managed Gene Ammons and Sonny Stitt before that. Carpenter's name is known from many music books, where he is listed as composer of the standard "Walkin'" (which is in fact probably a head arrangement by Miles Davis). Chet had been introduced to Carpenter by Dameron. On first impression, it seemed a sensible step on the part of the disorganized trumpeter to have finally hired a manager. The gamble didn't pay off, however. On August 23, 25, and 29, Carpenter had Chet record about three hours of music. He then sold all the tapes to Prestige, without paying the musicians a dime—he didn't even pay for their travel expenses. Prestige released the material on five separate albums [*Groovin', Comin' On, Smokin', Cool Burnin',* and *Boppin'*]. The music on these five LPs was later reissued on three CDs: *Stairway to the Stars, On a Misty Night,* and *Lonely Star,* (Prestige

PRCD 24173-2, 24174-2 and 24172-2)]. None of these albums is really bad, none particularly good. And Carpenter credits himself for composing so much of the material that some suspicion is naturally aroused. It was apparently unknown to everyone but Carpenter, for instance, that he had written the bebop chestnut "Cherokee." A lot of Dameron's material is also covered: "Choose Now," "So Easy," "On a Misty Night," "The 490," "Romas," and "Bevan Beeps."

It is noteworthy that Prestige was apparently incapable of finding journalists to write liner notes for these five albums who had very much nice to say. Most of them make it clear that they find the playing of the sidemen— tenor George Coleman and pianist Kirk Lightsey, among them—more engaging than that of the leader. But, they hasten to add, it is at least better than what Baker was playing earlier. On the sleeve of *Comin' On Over* Bob Porter says of *Chet Baker Sings*: "Listening to those performances today, the whole thing seems like a terrible hoax." Similar remarks can be found in the notes to the other disks. In *Down Beat*'s Readers Poll this year Chet lands in 12th place. In the Critics Poll he has been ignored for years, and would continue to be for the remainder of his life. In August 1989, a year after his death, he was inducted into *Down Beat*'s Hall of Fame with a meager seventeen votes.

Some months after this marathon session, Chet moved to Los Angeles, with a two-week stopover in Denver to play with his old partner Phil Urso. He later told interviewers that he left New York in order to escape the clutches of 'bean counters' like Carpenter. He has seen the Prestige records lying in the display windows and immediately got in the car with his family to get as far away from New York as fast as he could. This story does-n't quite accord with reality, however. Chet's relocation to California is reported as fact already in the liner notes to *Smokin'*—the first in the series of Prestige albums to be released. Maybe Carpenter didn't pay Chet because of debts to Carpenter that Chet had incurred. Maybe Chet had gotten advance word of the deal with Prestige, and that was enough for him to move to California. In any event, he had certainly settled there before the records were in the stores.

Meanwhile, the money has to come from somewhere. Chet is still using, and on top of everything else he now has another child: his son Paul was born in New York in 1965. Now he finds himself in Los Angeles with Carol, the toddler Dean, and the new baby Paul, broke. In July Carol gives birth to their third child together: Chet's only daughter, Melissa (usually called Missy).

Chet is faced with a difficult decision. Soon after reach-ing Los Angeles, at the end of 1965, an offer for a series of commercial records comes in: four with The Mariachi Brass, a Herb Alpert-style orchestra, consisting of studio musicians brought together by telephone,* and two with the Carmel Strings.† Chet consents, and in the next three years he is also co-soloist on five recordings of pop

*A *Taste of Tequila* (World Pacific 1839, WPS 21839)

† *Quietly There* (World Pacific WP 1847, WPS 21847) and *Into My Life* (WP 1858, WPS 21858)

hits produced by Bud Shank,* and a record with Joe Pass besides.† With two more similar LPs under his own name, it is altogether fourteen commercial productions. Most appear, awkwardly enough, on the Pacific Label—now called World Pacific—on which Chet had scored his first successes years earlier. And the producer is, again, Dick Bock. They are dreadful records, but it is not true—as many have claimed—that not a single note of jazz can be heard on them. Chet honestly strives to make the best of his infrequent solos. He himself later characterized the records as 'outrageous, terrible.' Bud Shank, who, since his first studio session with Chet in 1953 had developed into a dependable studio musician, is less hard on them: "Oh, I wasn't very picky. You had no choice then. We simply had to make those commercial records. We needed the money. At that time, in the second half of the '60s, nobody was making jazz records. Not Chet, not me, not anyone. And if I hadn't accepted this work, I wouldn't have made any records at all. It's that simple. We were glad that we could still earn something making music. I was not ashamed of the records, but I wasn't proud of them either. It was simply a job to pay the rent."

In the event, only the first record of the Mariachi Brass series is successful. The others sell only moderately

---

*California Dreamin' (World Pacific WP 1845, WPS 21845); Brazil! Brazil! Brazil! (WP 1855, WPS 21855); Michelle (WP 1840, WPS 21840); Magical Mystery (WP 1873, WPS 21873); Shank/Baker (ABC/ Paramount 77857)

† A Sign of the Times (World Pacific WP 1844, WPS 21844)

well—it seems the public has not been waiting for jazz musicians to cover pop songs. Chet's last commercial record, *Blood, Chet and Tears*, contains insipid covers of "Something," "Spinning Wheel," etc. It hardly sells at all. He has now recorded ten commercial records in quick succession, but the money is soon depleted.

At the beginning of 1966, Chet is arrested for drug offenses. In the first months of the following year he has to appear before a court in California to answer charges of document forgery. He has issued himself prescriptions in order to get narcotics again. He has to serve a term of several months. While involved in these judicial entanglements, his father—Chesney Henry Baker, Sr.,—dies in San Jose, in 1967.

Around this time Chet has one of the worst experiences of his eventful life. His own version of the incident is as follows. After one of his rare gigs, he is headed home when five hulking youths suddenly surround him in an abandoned street. They are toughs who his dealer has set upon him. Chet has not paid his bills, the dealer has undoubtedly threatened force, and now it's payback time. Chet is badly hurt. Not only does he lose his dope money, but—what is much worse—his teeth are damaged. He would later qualify the extent of the injury by pointing out that his teeth were already in bad shape, then add: "They finished them off."

Chet in *Jazz Hot* (November 1983): "In 1969 my other front tooth was lost. But my teeth were already in bad condition through all the drugs anyway. I got a denture, and when I tried to play again, I could get no sound out my trumpet. So I gave it up. I worked almost two years in a gas station, 16 hours a day." In *Let's Get Lost* he says: "I was on welfare for a while, then I got a job in a gas station from seven o'clock in the morning until eleven at night in San Jose and did that for a few months, meanwhile continuing to try to find a way to play with these dentures."

Carol's version is as follows: "It happened in July 1966, two or three days after Melissa's birth. No, not later. Melissa was a few days old, that I'm sure of. Chet had a gig in a club in San Francisco. He had just been paid and went on the street to his car when five black guys surrounded him. They had already tried the evening before that to rob him, but they failed. So they tried it again, and they were so furious at him that after they took the money they started to kick him. They beat him and kicked him between the legs, on the legs, they gave him two black eyes, and they hit him in the mouth. I was shocked when I saw him the next morning. For two or three years afterward Chet couldn't play a note. He became a real family man. For a while we lived on welfare. At the end of 1966 he got a denture, paid for by someone at a record company. I think it was Dick Bock. Did Chet have a job at a gas station? Yes, one evening, no more. It was his idea. I thought it was nice of him, but he said, 'Forget about it.' He could not stand that kind of work, anyway. He would go nuts."

In fact, it is unlikely that Chet got his dentures in the summer of 1966. He was still active in the latter half of that year. He made at least two more records after July, and two more were possibly recorded in the same period. But it is certain that he was beaten up in the summer of

1966. In its August 20, 1966 issue, *Melody Maker* reports: "Chet Baker was seriously injured in San Francisco last week when he became innocently involved in an ugly, interracial incident . . . Baker was walking home after headlining the show at the Trident, in Sausalito, a San Francisco suburb.

" 'I was just trying to get a taxi,' he says, 'when five guys surrounded me and started to beat me up. Ironically it was two colored guys who'd saved me after I'd tried to escape by getting into a car with four of five white kids who first threw me back in the street. The hoodlums beat me some more until these two colored guys told them to stop and took me to the hospital . . . They also smashed a part of a tooth off.' "

These last words are important: Chet didn't lose 'all his front teeth,' as some journalists have claimed, or even just one tooth—but only a part of one tooth. Not a pleasant thing to have happen, but it doesn't seem to have hampered his playing too much at the time. Baker went on performing and recording until the condition of his teeth deteriorated to the point where—probably in the second half of 1968 or early 1969—he was forced to have them all removed, and was fitted with a denture. This is a big change for any trumpet player.

In April 1968 he was still recording—the album *Magical Mystery* with Bud Shank, which consists of uninspired Beatles covers—and then the curtain falls. The next record would be the unfortunate *Albert's House*, in 1969, on which his technique is at its absolute nadir.* The only

*Repertoire REP 4167; PAR-200 F-CD

other recording from the period 1969–1973 is *Blood, Chet and Tears*, which was recorded in April or July of 1970.*

Chet stops playing completely at this point and moved with his family into his mother's house in San Jose. Carol and his mother have to raise the family with the welfare check: 320 dollars a month and 130 dollars in food stamps. Chet, completely depressed, does nothing but hang around his mother's house and get high. Again, he forges prescriptions for heroin. He is arrested. Now, he is extremely anxious. This is the second time in the US he is charged with forging prescriptions. Others have been condemned to long terms in San Quentin for such offenses. But Chet is lucky. The judge is a former trumpet player, and releases Chet after five month's detention on condition that he enter a methadone program. Chet would remain on the methadone program for seven years.

When Chet is released at the end of 1969, he takes stock and makes some levelheaded decisions. Since singing and playing trumpet are the only things he knows how to do, he has to devote himself to them again. He must re-learn how to play the trumpet. And so he gets hold of an instrument—the flugelhorn has disappeared in the meantime—and begins to practice. With great effort (and it shows), he manages to produce the records *Albert's House* and *Blood, Chet and Tears*. For four or five years, he makes no public appearances.

---

* There is some confusion as to the date of this recording. An earlier edition of Sjøgren's discography says 'probably April, 1970', which is later changed to 'July 6, 1970'. The sampler 'Jazz on Verve' gives July 5, 1970. Considering Chet's condition, it is likely that it took him more than a day to record the LP. Sjøgren mentions no other recordings in 1970, and no recordings at all in 1971 and 1972.

two weeks at
the half note:
the comeback

*C*arol Baker: "From 1969 to 1975 Chet was clean. The whole time he took nothing but methadone, nothing else, believe me. He became a real family man. He loved his kids, he really cared about his kids. That began to change when he started with the heroin again. The jazz scene and all that traveling was responsible. It alienated him from his family."

It may be that Carol is a little too fond in her recollections. Anyone who needs methadone for that long can't have kicked the habit completely. And is Chet really the family man now he purports to be? He is more domestic during this than during any other time of his life. But he has also inaugurated a relationship with Diana Vavra, whom he already knew in 1970—if not before.

Chet in *Let's Get Lost*: "Diane and Carol know each other because Diane used to baby-sit for us in 1970, '71. The first time I saw Diane she was playing drums with no shoes on in a pizza parlor where they had kind of jam sessions every Sunday . . . And ever since then we've been tight."

Diane in *Let's Get Lost*: "I loved Chet way before I met him, because for me he personified the very thing that gave meaning to my life, and that is jazz. He looked like a Greek god to me, and I fell in love with him immediately. He was very gentle, very sweet, very charming. I guess that's what it was. The mystique about him."

Because an unemployed musician with a family can't always afford drugs, Chet sometimes drinks too much in this period. Three times—in 1971, 1972, and 1975—he is charged with drunk driving. During this 'domestic' period, Chet tries to write his memoirs. Carol: "He wrote a full stack of paper. That was the end of the '60s, the beginning of the '70s. But then he lost the memoirs, they vanished when he went on trips. He wrote very well. He had a way of putting words together that astonished me. He didn't write off the top of his head, he thought before he picked up a pen."

Chet in 1983: "In recent years many people have asked whether I would want to write a book. I tried it several times, in 1974 for example, and I wrote something like 300,000 words! But writing, that really isn't my profession" (*Jazz Hot*). More then ten years after Chet's death, editors at *Spin* magazine sent Carol a fragment of this material to authenticate. She published it in 1997 under the title *As though I had wings: the lost memoir*. With creative layout the book is stretched to a little over a hundred dred pages, and contains information about Chet's life from 1946 to 1963. Much of it deals with his adventures in the army and his subsequent drug use. Though not always reliable, it confirms Carol's impression overall:

Chet in Toronto, mid-70s.

© Paul J. Hoeffler

At the beginning of 1974 Chet sent for Carol and the children to New York, where he wanted to settle again. But the family didn't get any peace. When the people in their neighborhood discover that Chet had been in prison for drug possession, they make their life a living hell. The family moves to Long Island. Chet, Carol, and the children live there two months, when an article appears in the paper, depicting his drug past in the most lurid colors. After the article appeared, according to Carol, every night thirty or forty children would come by on their bicycles and pelt Chet and their kids with garbage. When Carol goes out shopping, she is also attacked. The adults in the neighborhood do nothing to stop this vandalism and harassment. The Bakers finally decamp to a hotel with a few suitcases. Carol thinks she remembers that her kids, in revenge, let loose the dozen or so mice that they kept in a cage.

When the family returned to the motel after a meal, they were told that they could vacate immediately. A mouse, which had apparently managed to slip into their luggage, had been found, and the management of the hotel refused to lodge the family any longer. A couple of months later Chet moved in with his new girlfriend— and then these problems, at least, came to an end.

During this time—March and April 1974—he played with Gene Roland's Jazz Adventure Orchestra, and again at the Half Note. Lee Konitz was enchanted by the born-again trumpeter. Konitz: "In New York in 1974 Chet and I tried to get a group together. For all sorts of reasons nothing much came of the group. We did a concert in Ornette Coleman's Loft that was recorded and issued later by India Navigation. Chet didn't feel so good that day. It was obvious that he had no desire to play. So the record doesn't give such a good picture of his playing at that time.

"I had the impression that Chet always had a certain ego problem. When we played together, he believed that I wanted to determine the style of music. That I wanted to be the leader. That wasn't the case at all, but it hurt our collaboration. So I think there was something unmusical going on between us."

Bud Shank: "I think that Chet was unsure of himself then. The direction of jazz had changed while he was away. I never noticed much of an ego problem myself. But I know that something similar often happens with people who are outwardly very quiet. Chet was like that. He didn't speak much. He was turned in on himself. So he was as a young man, and so he was after his come-back. It was difficult for him to express himself. Every contact, in fact, was a problem for him. Such people often start to take drugs because they think that no one respects them. Or because they think that they are not outgoing enough. Then they land in a chemical never-never land."

In the summer 1974, Chet got an offer to make a few records for the CTI label. The producer of this young label, Creed Taylor, didn't want to bring out bootlegs of low budget sessions, only first-class records with first-class musicians, in deluxe packaging. On the three CTI records to which Chet contributes between July 1974 and April 1975—*She Was Too Good to Me*, a reunion concert with Mulligan in Carnegie Hall, and *Concierto*, led by Jim Hall—veterans like Chet, Mulligan, Paul Desmond, and Jim Hall are teamed with the hot young jazzmen of the period: John Scofield, Steve Gadd, Bob James (on the Fender Rhodes, because that was also fashionable), and the inevitable Ron Carter. With this formula Taylor hoped to reach both the older and the younger audience.

Chet believed that he was now solidly established with CTI, and told one interviewer that he intended his next album to feature scat singing, like he attempted as early as 1958 on parts of *It Could Happen to You*—but now with multiple track technology, so that several voices could be heard at once. In an interview in 1986 Chet came back to the idea, but it was never realized.*

Why didn't Chet really make it in the US after his comeback? He seemed to fall between two stools. For conservative jazz fans and musicians, he was too introverted, had too few show-business qualities. Fans of progressive jazz, on the other hand, were put off by his trumpet sound and skin color. There is no doubt that Chet was partly the victim of reverse discrimination. Black Nationalism was its height in certain circles. Cool Jazz was invented in order to 'whitewash' jazz and efface its Afro-American origin. "Baker's approach is superficial. Chet expresses himself within the limits of a restricted emotional span. It is a theater, from which all passions are banished, an art with a prohibition of all vibrant

Jazz Press, September 17, 1975; *The Wire*, November 1985

colors. Since his West Coast period, Chet, like every other musician of this trend, has become completely obscure. So far as the jazz public is concerned, Baker and his ilk have become (in the words of Orwell) 'unpersons.' "*

Ria Wigt of Wim Wigt Productions: "The American jazz musicians with whom I have spoken didn't think too highly of Chet in the '70s and the '80s. They weren't exactly pleased that we got involved with such a person. It had a lot to do with black and white. Chet once had more success than Miles Davis, and that was his fault. Years later, when Chet got more work in Europe, that was more cause for jealousy. Everyone knew that Chet sometimes didn't show up, and yet got invited back again and again. Now, I can understand that. Others had to fight for every gig. The more established artists also wanted to hear nothing about him. Chet didn't live by their values. Their values were: making a lot of money, having a big car, living in a nice house, doing fancy concerts. Everywhere a string of concerts, festivals, and jazz parties. Then you've made it. Then the script calls for phrases like 'He's a very good friend of mine,' or 'He's a beautiful person'—words that mean absolutely nothing. Chet was always an anti-hero. He said it over and over: 'I don't go to the States anymore.' Especially in his last years. He only wanted a little money, an agreeable life, his drugs, and a little acknowledgement."

*Rudy Koopmans (ed.) *Jazz/Improvisation in the Context of a Growing Minority* (Amsterdam 1977)

Gerrie Teekens, owner of the record company Criss Cross: "Chet got little work in New York. Later, when he was in Europe more and more frequently, then he got none [in New York] at all any more. When he had gigs in the US, it was usually in California. He told me once: 'In Europe they look upon jazz as art. In America it's a diversion. Somebody opens a restaurant and installs another band off to the side. People don't listen.'"

Chet in *Jazz Hot*: "It's very hard to get regular work in the United States. If you play in a club in New York, you're not allowed to play in another club the month before or the month after. That's in the contract. So I have to travel. It's much simpler to travel in Europe, and there's more work. It's also much more relaxed here and the level of perception is much higher than in the States. There the average listener has the mentality of a twelve-year-old."

Carol Baker: "In America the emphasis is on scandal, publicity, glamour. In Europe they see things more clearly. There the people have the patience to listen to his music and are not so dazzled by externals."

For many Americans, Chet's high point was in the Mulligan Quartet, and his later music represents Chet in decline. Bud Shank put it the most diplomatically. "His playing? I found it marvelous to listen to him and to play with him. The tragedy is that he stopped developing when he became addicted. We lost a star. We will never know what he could have achieved otherwise. Did he play differently later? Well, you probably have to play differently when you lose all your teeth. No, since the '50s

it's all gone downhill for him." Further questioning dis-
closed that Shank had heard Chet only twice since his
comeback. But he still held to his opinion. "That's all
there is to it, as everyone knows."

In July 1975, two months after the *Concierto* session,
Chet traveled to Europe. His stay in Europe would last
much longer than Carol expected. It marked the defini-
tive end of Chet's family life. Carol Baker: "It all started
with the woman whom he met in 1974 in a club in New
York. Ruth Young was her name. She brought Chet back
to heroin. From then on, everything went wrong. If you
take heroin, you use all your money and energy to get
hold of the stuff. Then, you get sick—it's a vicious circle.
There was nothing I could do about it. I let him go. He
was sick. I never got mad at him. We have never officially divorced. And we never said goodbye to each other.
Chet left in 1975 and since then I've been free of him. It
should have been a normal tour, but he left and didn't
come back. He only returned seventeen months later.
Then I knew he was addicted again. You also have to
know, when Chet took heroin, he could be manipulated
very easily. He had no will of his own. He was a victim of
the jazz scene and his friends. Later Ruth vanished, and
Diane arrived. That was another one like Ruth. Carved
from the same wood."

Jacques Pelzer, too, denies that one can speak of a real
break between Carol and Chet: "Ruth Young? Everyone
probably slips once. He could never be parted from
Carol, and that is remarkable. He said to me: 'I will
always love Carol.' But he had a little adventure here and
there, like everyone else. Nothing to speak of. Chet
remained loyal to Carol."

Nevertheless, the relationship with Ruth Young, with interruptions, would last a long time. And at the beginning of the '80s Diane Vavra became his steady companion on his European tours. Diane had to give way to Ruth again when Chet was in New York. Gerrie Teekens has met both women: "Ruth Young is a crafty woman. She certainly has a ready tongue. When I was in New York in 1982, to make a record with Warne Marsh, Chet was living with her. A short time later I heard he sold her piano—saying that she couldn't play piano anyway—and her fur coat. That was the last straw. She ended it then. Diane was not exactly 'another one like Ruth.' Ruth was biting and could be venomous when she wanted to be. Diane was much nicer. Much softer. She was a dear girl. She took care of him well. I admire her for staying with him—with someone with so unpredictable a temper."

Ruth Young on vocals with Nicola Stilo on flute.
© Cecco Maino

In the years 1974–1976 Chet often let his beard grow. He combed his long, dark hair straight back. Together with Ruth—in long curls, gigantic sunglasses, and South American poncho—they made a genuine hippie couple.

In *Let's Get Lost* Ruth gives an account of herself: "When I first met Chet, he was very unhealthy and a lot more vulnerable than he ultimately became, because he was on the rebound of his career. He was on the outs trying to get back in. And he was a lot nicer, and a lot more fun to be around—if you can ever say such a thing. But it was because of his insecurity of himself that things were quite different."

Ruth came from a show-biz family. Jane Russell and Marilyn Monroe were supposedly friends of her parents. At home, Chet's records were often on because her mother idolized him. By the time Ruth and he met, the early luster had long worn off. But he still had 'something': "I met him at the Half Note . . . Eventually he walked in, and headed for the bandstand, and nothing was said, but we glanced at each other. I watched him throughout his performance, and he was gaunt, and he looked terrible and he was wearing that red and burgundy combination that he thought was such a big hit, which was wild, with a pair of cowboy boots. He looked absolutely horrible, but still, he was charming. It was still my hero walking in the room . . . I had to thank him. I said something like, 'Hey, I got to tell you, it's great to see you. I think you're doing a hell of a job', 'cause he sounded like shit. He was trying so hard and that's what was so endearing—to see this man completely reveal himself. To look so horrible, to sound so terrible, but to be standing there, and trying, and that was the moment I connected with him. And he said, 'Well you know, that's really nice to hear,' and all this stuff, and it was real cute and then he said, 'Well, don't be a stranger,' so I went back the next night and that was it. Then we just started hanging out like permanently from that time. So it took like exactly twenty seconds to get hooked."

Chet in *Let's Get Lost*, of Ruth: "Ruth was a very vivacious lady, open, made friends easily, quick to smile, and an intelligent girl. She loved to dance and sing. And we got together and we hung out for a few years, six, seven years. And all during that time I tried to get her to sing with the band, you know . . . We had a record to do in Milano and we recorded this tune . . . Oh, it's such a beautiful thing. 'Whatever Possessed Me.' And I got her to sing on the record on that tune."*

Some weeks after arriving in Europe in July 1975, Chet played at the jazz festival in Laren, northern Holland. It is his first appearance in Holland since his Amsterdam visit with Dick Twardzik twenty years earlier. The concert draws little attention. Maarten Derksen, employed at that time with manager Wim Wigt: "The public looked rather stunned. Chet sat there in a silly striped T-shirt, with his hollow cheeks. I interviewed him the next morning. He had a woman with him [Diane], a small fashionable woman with dark curls. At first I thought she was his

The Incredible Chet Baker Plays and Sings (Carosello 25075), March 1977

wife. He claimed that he only took methadone and was completely off heroin. He didn't look too well, but he was coherent. 'I get the audience that had earlier been to hear Miles Davis,' he said."

Chet wasn't at his best in Laren, because he had not played in ten days and instead had hung out with Jacques Pelzer. In the small Italian town of Citta di Castello, he nearly took off George Wein, the festival organizer's, head with his trumpet. Wein ducked, and the trumpet landed on the ground, totaled. "I said to George Wein, 'Take this festival and suck it.' Then I grabbed my trumpet and threw it at his head, as hard as I could. A marvelous instrument. It was the first time in my life that I did something like that. But I just couldn't stand the situation. I wanted to play, but it was simply impossible. The festival was disgracefully organized."*

Jules Deelder: "In 1975 I saw him in a club in Rotterdam for the first time live. He was much darker than I expected; his beard was downright black. Motionlessly, he sat on a barstool, turned completely in on himself. He played with a certain Belgian guy [Pelzer], who continuously noodled on his flute, although he had a good alto sax standing by him the whole time. The drummer didn't show at all. Hardly ideal circumstances for playing. Chet's trumpet playing wasn't sensational either then, but it made no difference to me. I found it just so crazy that he was sitting there in front of me! When he first opened his mouth and began to sing—I think it was "You Don't Know What Love Is"—I felt like ice-cold water

*Jazz Press, September 17, 1975

was running down my back, exactly like twenty years before at a party with my sister. Although it had become a little fragile, his voice had lost nothing of its magic."

At the end of 1975 and in 1976, Wim and Ria Wigt organized some concerts for Chet. In the course of the tour Chet was arrested in Germany. Ria Wigt: "We already had him playing in Germany, and it had caused no problems. He was scheduled to play in Burghausen, near Salzburg. This time everything went wrong. Customs alerted the police, and shortly before he was to go on stage he was arrested. What had happened? We had not bothered to get authorization for Chet to return to Germany. Chet had been deported from there sometime back in the '60s. The ban was still in effect. In fact, that seemed to be the case in several countries. Chet hadn't informed us of it. He only said that he wanted to play in Germany again. Of course he thought, That was such a long time ago . . . So Chet had to go back into the clink. Not long, only a few days, as I recall . . . "

the high-class
hobo: back in
europe

*b*y 1976, little was left of the good looks that Chet had known how to maintain for such a long time. Well into the '60s, with a multitude of prison terms behind him and masses of heroin in his veins, Chet still had something of the All-American Boy about him. His change in life seemed not to affect him. But on the covers of the 1974 albums, *She Was Too Good to Me* and the reunion album with Mulligan, the skin has visibly tightened around his cheekbones. Then the decline proceeds quickly. Heroin deprives him of his appetite. A year later, in Laren, his cheeks have shrunk alarmingly. At a second concert in Laren, in February 1976, it seems as if he could collapse at any moment. At the end of 1976, when he returns to the States, he had become a hopeless junkie again and was wrinkled like an old Native American. In December of this year he turned 47. Still, in good times—like he can be seen on a video from June 1985—he often appears amazingly youthful.*

---

*June 30, 1985, *Candy* (Sonet Film A B Schweden, USA Music Video)

In many of his concerts, he was accompanied by Harold Danko, who continued to play with him after an initial tour. Chet met up with old friends again and often stayed with Jacques Pelzer. He would remain in Europe for a year and a half, until December 1976.

There is not much public interest yet. Between concerts there are long periods of inactivity, and the European record companies are initially uninterested. For the time being, the interest of the American labels remains stronger. Chet and Ruth go back to New York. Pelzer goes too, and regularly plays with Chet in Stryker's Bar. Chet also visits Carol and his children that winter. Supposedly, he gives them a scare. Since his departure, he has aged noticeably.

In February 1977, he makes an album for Ornette Coleman's Artists House label and one for A&M Records. *Once Upon a Summertime* sounds like a Miles album from the '60s. Oddly, the record is not released until 1980. The other one, *You Can't Go Home Again*, creates more interest than all other records since his comeback. He plays here with jazz-rock luminaries such as Michael Brecker, Alphonso Johnson, and (again) Ron Carter. In March and April, Chet, Ruth, and Jacques Pelzer are back in Europe. Chet plays mainly in France and makes a curious recording in Milan—the only record on which he can be heard playing with Ruth, who is obviously a talented singer. The pianist is the Frenchman Michel Graillier, later one of Chet's regular sidemen.

In May, he returns to New York to record some additional tracks for *You Can't Go Home Again*. And he is invited to participate as singer and trumpeter on one number of a record by Astrud Gilberto. The period June 1977 –October 1978 is little documented. Chet is still in the States, lives with Ruth or his family, has a few gigs here and there and leads an inconspicuous life otherwise. The CTI label doesn't call. Only in 1982 do they offer him just two (moderately successful) recording opportunities, one of them as a sideman. The attempts to launch him as star have apparently not borne much financial fruit. His long absence in Europe is undoubtedly to blame. Fortunately, he is popular enough now in Europe to undertake a tour with a regular rhythm section. Around November 1st he kicks off a two-month tour with pianist Phil Markowitz, bass player Scott Lee, and drummer Jeff Brillinger. Markowitz, with his intense, but unobtrusive playing and harmonic refinement, is an ideal companion for Chet. The tour lasts until the end of the year. The bass player meanwhile has been replaced with a young Belgian: Jean-Louis Rassinfosse. When the tour is over, Chet again decides to remain in Europe. This time, his residence in Europe acquires a more or less permanent character. For obvious reasons. While in America he can-not—or just barely—make a living, in Europe the inter-est in his music has grown steadily—particularly in France, Italy, Germany, and Denmark.

And from now on there is no lack of work. The concerts follow in quick succession, and there is increasing time in the studio. During these years a number of small labels started by jazz aficionados start up. Chet appears to make himself available to just about any of them for roughly the sum of $1000. In 1979 he makes eleven

Philip Catherine.

© Jacky Lepage

records. In 1980 he makes ten. They are put out by companies like Sandra (Stuttgart), Circle (Cologne) and Steeplechase (Copenhagen). He also becomes associated with musicians who understand his music: pianist Enrico Pieranunzi, guitarist Philip Catherine, and bassists Rassinfosse, Ricardo Del Fra and Niels-Henning Ørsted-Pedersen. The collaboration with Graillier intensifies, and by 1983 he is Chet's regular pianist. In 1981 Chet meets Leo Mitchell, an American drummer, who lives alternately in Italy and New York.

Philip Catherine: "I played with Chet for the first time in 1981. His playing had something magical. It was a fantastic concert, although at first I didn't want to play with

him at all. I thought he was only a mediocre musician—
a spent veteran, living off his former fame. The guy had
a bad reputation at the time. The second concert took
place in Switzerland. After twenty minutes, it started to
go so well that I got into a kind of trance. It was as if
everything was going by itself. Was it difficult to play
with him? It was easy and hard at the same time. On the
one hand, what he wanted was quite clear. He had outstanding timing, and harmonically no questions were left
open. One only had to follow him. It also sounded so
nice. He had a beautiful sound. You could never get
enough of it. On the other hand, I wasn't very familiar
with his repertoire. I was making a lot of rock-style
records at the time. He played the jazz standards, and at
the beginning of the '80s that was not my strong suit.
Chet was notorious for rarely arranging things with his
sidemen beforehand. He just sat down and started to
blow. Fortunately, he never did that with me. I said right
off at the first concert, 'Chet, if you want to play something that I don't know, you have to rehearse it with me
briefly.' And so he always chose things that we all knew.
At the start, that wasn't much fun, because my repertoire
wasn't very big yet. Yeah, one time he threw in a piece
that we didn't know, neither me nor Jean-Louis
Rassinfosse. He ended up sitting there and playing
alone. I think he was in a bad mood that evening. A
strange idea.

"It was also difficult sometimes to be always playing
without drummers. Especially during his slow ballads.
But because he had such good timing, it still came off.
Whenever I had problems with the tempo, I'd hear him

saying very quietly: 'Tschick-tschick-tschick-tschick'—
exactly the accents of the hi-hat.

"I liked to use electronics in concerts—any possible way
of playing with sound. After a few evenings I wanted to
try it at least once. It worked very well. Chet never complained about it. He came on stage one night and saw me
with all my pedals and buttons and so forth. 'Wow,' he
said under his breath. That was all. He gave me complete
freedom.

"He was definitely one of my influences, along with
Django Reinhardt and the pop guitarist Jeff Beck.
Django was my first ideal. I adopted something of his
timing and song-like sound. Chet has influenced me in
matters of phrasing and tone production. He's completely a musician for whom feeling is foremost. That's always
been clear to me, even during the time I was spending
seven hours a day doing finger exercises."

In the United States, the trumpeter had little work in the
'80s. Sometimes he appeared with Phil Markowitz, Leo
Mitchell, and Bob Mover. He hardly made an overpow-
ering impression at the few concerts in the States at
which he does appear. The few record offers he got he
usually turned down; he was too proud to hire himself
out for a thousand dollars in his native land, site of his
former glory. In Europe he was less demanding.

Bud Shank: "I saw Chet again for the first time in a long
time in New York in 1981. I was playing in the city with
another group and passed by the club where he was
appearing, Fat Tuesday's. He was just back from France.
He had to go directly from the airport to the gig. He said

Chet, Niels-Henning, Ørsted Pedersen and Doug Raney at Montmartre, Copenhagen, 1979.

© Jørgen Bo

that he didn't feel especially well, and asked me whether I would help him through it by sitting in for a little. So I joined him and played. The concert was broadcast over the air. Someone sent me a tape of the evening half a year ago, but I still haven't found time to listen to it. Chet looked awful, I do remember that."

In April 1981, Chet traveled to New York, but a few weeks later resumed the unending tour of Europe. Still, he spent the greater part of 1982, the winter of 1984–85, the end of December 1985, January 1986, and the first half of 1987 in the States. He favored the winter months, because of the mild Californian climate. He had friends there who could put him up, and Diane's stepfather lived there as well. Carol, in the meantime, had moved in with

Chet's mother in Stillwater, Oklahoma. The distance between Chet and his family had grown steadily greater. Carol Baker tried to come to terms with it.

Carol: "Perhaps it should have been that way. Maybe he would not have given the world so much music if he had stayed at home. Because in the last years he played more frequently than ever, made more records than ever. It seemed as if everyone in Europe wanted to hear him. He made many people happy with his music. That's how I try and look at it. Maybe he never could have done that here in Oklahoma."

In *Let's Get Lost* she says: "He just leaves as he comes, which is okay. It's always a little bit of a surprise, you know, when you've planned dinner or something, and you've just been to the market and spent a few bucks on groceries and you come home and he's gone, you know. What am I going to do with all this food now?"

I talked with Carol several times. Initially, she was a little curt; that soon changed, however, and then she spoke very freely. Her favorite theme: What a gentle and sensitive person Chet was, and how she could not prevent him from starting up with the drugs again. She seemed compelled to absolve both Chet and herself, even though I hadn't expressed the least reproach. Carol: "In 1982 I moved with the children from New York to Oklahoma. It made no sense to stay in New York. Chet had to travel in order to be able to work as a musician, there was nothing you could do about it. So why should we stay in the big, dangerous city anymore? Oklahoma is a much healthier environment for the children. More space. We moved into the house of Chet's mother in Stillwater."

None of Chet's four children plays an instrument. What has become of Chet's first son, Chesney? Carol: "I don't know much about him. He keeps to himself and likes to move around a lot. Once in a great while he calls, but otherwise I don't hear from him. He wasn't at the funeral either."

Peter Huijts: "I met all three of his children from his third marriage. They were in their 20s then. They all have something of Chet. His son Paul has something of the arrogance that Chet had. Chet's daughter has something of the temper that Chet could display. And his eldest son Dean is the dear, sweet boy that Chet also was."

In *Let's Get Lost* Bruce Weber asks Chet's daughter Missy, "If you were to take a vacation with him, what would it be like and where would you go?" Missy: "Mmm, probably a cruise, because he couldn't get off the ship. He couldn't disappear. For a few days we'd be able to track him down somewhere. To an island, you know, a small island. That would probably be the best vacation."

Diane Vavra told Weber: "He's so obsessed with getting high that he can't have a, quote, 'normal kind of life'. He just can't. That really is his first priority, getting high. And you can't have a family, you can't have a home and still get high every day. It's too expensive, for one thing. He knows that and he's told me time and time again . . . he's going to stop. He will stop. 'Can't you see? I'm not using as much as I was before. You know, give me some slack. I'll stop'. But we both know he's not going to stop. We're playing a game with pretend. He's pretending that he is going to stop and I'm pretending that he's going to stop."

It is notable that in his later years Chet could always escape the police despite his junkie lifestyle and appearance. His last arrest in America in connection with narcotics took place in 1969. He never committed a crime, like burglary, to get drugs. When the money ran out, he resorted to Pelzer, later to other friends, who gave him food and housing. Chet never dealt drugs either; everything he bought was for his own consumption.

Peter Huijts was continually surprised at how friendly and charming Chet could be while eluding customs officials. He was careful to carry only small quantities with him, or nothing at all. If he went to a country with an especially strict drug policy, he took nothing with him and shopped on the spot. He became the high-class hobo, the world traveler who lived out of his suitcase and in general did whatever he wanted to do.

Bass player Harry Emmery: "Chet loved driving cars and never seemed to get tired of it. He drove in his own car to the gigs. He didn't hesitate to sit for twelve straight hours behind the wheel. He tore around the streets at a frightful pace."

In *Let's Get Lost* Chet is asked about the happiest day of his life. "Oh my goodness . . . Maybe the day I got my Alfa Romeo SS. It was a nice day, and I had a lot of fun . . . It was only 1300cc, but it would run along at 125mph. But it was just so low off the ground that it made it seem like you were really flying. Nice car."

Evert Hekkema: "Chet became a real cosmopolitan. He coped with languages well. He could make himself understood anywhere. He spoke fluent Italian, without any accent. In a few seconds, he could calculate what a certain sum in dollars was in Marks, francs, lire, or guilders."

Jacques Pelzer: "When Chet got out of prison in 1962 he spoke Italian perfectly, just as good as English. Later he also learned French quite well. He was highly intelligent. He could read the thoughts of other people. He was never uncertain. Always perfect control, even over himself. At the wheel too, in the car. He could have become a taxi driver anywhere. He knew every city."

Harry Emmery: "Chet had the spirit of 1992 years before then. European borders didn't exist for him. He once called me from Italy to ask whether I wanted to play a concert with him in France the next night. They were lonely concerts and lonely tours. He was very taciturn, I was very taciturn. We mainly saw each other on stage. I don't know if I could have endured more than the few short tours I did with Chet. It was a rather wretched life despite the money. During the day, he slept. In the late afternoon he went out in search of drugs. And in the evening he sat entranced on stage.

"Once it looked as if we were going to divide a room. We had a gig in Switzerland. I arrived at the hotel, and it turned out that no room had been reserved for me. The others were all taken. Chet suggested that we share a bed. Later he changed his mind; he would sleep in the room with Micheline Pelzer and Michel Graillier, who were playing with us. It was clear to him that we came from two completely different worlds. The next morning I wanted to call him for breakfast. I opened the door, and there they lay—Chet, Micheline, and Michel, all in one bed. It smelled rather musty in the room, everything was in chaos. I immediately thought to myself, Just get out of here. This is definitely not your scene."

in search of chet baker:
the interview(s)

*i*t was not very hard to interview Chet. He was clear and sober throughout our conversation. Tom Mandersloot, owner of the Amsterdam music clubs De Kroeg and De Stip, had given me some advice beforehand. (Chet stayed with him fairly often in the autumn 1987.) "You better not talk about drugs," he had said, "because then he might immediately break the conversation off." No wonder—this is the man who was hounded his entire life on the subject by the tabloid press.

The problem was rather how to find him, and how to make an appointment he would keep. The interview finally took place on Thursday September 24, 1987 around 3:30 in the afternoon in the jazz club De Stip ('The Spot').

Attempts to track him down had begun two months earlier, when it was announced that Chet would play a festival in Hilversum. Evidently he was in Europe again after having been in the US for a while, and having completed a successful tour of Japan. I immediately called the Wim Wigt Agency and got his employee Jacqueline van Hattum on the line. "Chet is always missing," she said, and sighed. "He has no solid residence, and if he would only say what hotel he is staying in . . ." Chet, it was clear, was her problem child. "I can reserve rooms, as many as you like, but then he often just checks in somewhere else and forgets to report. We had agreed to stay in contact, because Wim organizes nearly all his concerts. We even had to call the airport once to find out where he was. If only he wasn't in such demand . . . "

Evert Hekkema suggested I call Jacques Pelzer. There was—besides Diane, of course—nobody closer to him than Pelzer. Pelzer, therefore, must know where he is. I dialed the number and got a nice French-speaking man on the line. I had not met this eccentric pharmacist before and initially couldn't understand a word he was saying. After a while, it became clear that he speaks English with a marked French pronunciation. Chet was staying, according to him, somewhere in Paris. I got two telephone numbers: one at the hotel where he should be at the moment, one at the hotel that (in all likelihood) he would check into the following day.

In neither hotel has anyone heard of the American, even when I try to pronounce his name as French as I can. Shortly before the festival at which he is to perform, I get Wim Wigt's co-worker on the phone a couple more times. She tells me that Wigt has arranged another appearance two weeks later in De Kroeg. She assumes that Chet will spend the interim 'somewhere in Amsterdam.' For the time being, she has booked a hotel in Loosdrecht for him. No, she can't promise anything, but I can try maybe.

Chet seems this time to have actually checked into the

Rocky Knauer,
Antwerp,
October 1987.
© Jacky Lepage

designated hotel, together with Michel Graillier, the gui-
tarist/flutist Nicola Stilo, and bass player Joachim (Rocky)
Knauer—as usual, a completely different lineup from
the one announced for the concert. None of them can be

137

reached at their room, however—not in the afternoon nor in the evening shortly before the concert. The next morning they check out early.

I cannot attend the concert because of prior obligations, and I never discover where that 'somewhere in Amsterdam' is. I inquire fruitlessly with a lot of hotels in Amsterdam and await the concert in De Kroeg anxiously.

Two weeks later, the concert is at hand. I buy a ticket, and to my amazement Chet is already there. It is 10:30 at night, and he leans relaxed against the piano, a cigarette in the corner of his mouth. He is leafing through large sheets of music. Diane sits beside him on a high barstool. Considering his circumstances, he looks pretty good. The ever-present crowd that only show up to check out how wretched he will look this time must have gone home disappointed.

The concert begins promptly, but the conditions leave something to be desired: there is a superfluous echo in the trumpet, the vocals are barely audible—and it is brutally hot. During the ballads you can hear the bass of the pop music that is being piped into the lobby. After 45 minutes, Chet decides it is high time for a break to 'have a drink and dry off'. "We'll be back in fifteen minutes," he adds, wrongly. I go on stage and shake his hand. He nods to me kindly. Drops of perspiration glint in every furrow of his lined face. I mumble something about working for a big newspaper—which can't be taken too literally—and being a great admirer of his, then ask whether I can interview him in his hotel. "Of course," he says at once, "but we're not in a hotel. We're staying next door, with Tom and Linda Mandersloot. Come at one o'clock, how about that?"

"Oh, that's beautiful."

"I'll see you then."

"So—tomorrow at one?", I ask again, just to make sure. It's all going a little too fast for me.

"I'll be there," he assures me.

Then I'm introduced to Diane, who smiles and extends her hand, and leave the stage contented.

On the next day, no one answers my ring. Is Chet staying on another floor? Is the bell broken? He had said next door—did he mean the house between De Stip and De Kroeg? After half an hour, Linda comes out with a shopping bag. No, they had not heard the bell, they often oversleep, particularly if they've been up late the night before. And they had. Chet had played three sets, and afterward they had all been drinking until seven o'clock that morning. He has said nothing to her about an interview, but if I came back about 2:30 he was sure to be awake.

So I return after about an hour of strolling over the canals. Linda informs that there is still no one stirring upstairs. So I wait. About two hours later, Rocky Knauer, the very tall bassist, shows up. He is the only one who has slept in a hotel—Tom indicates that he is somewhat more careful with his money than the rest—and makes a very vibrant impression. He has just come from a long stiff walk, 'for his health.'

When Rocky is filled in, he goes straight up to check on the situation. He comes back alone. "They're all having breakfast, but even ten horses can't drag Chet out of bed," he reports. "Yes, the man is simply dead tired. After all, he is already approaching sixty. And the trips we make . . . typical Wim Wigt tours. Up and down Europe. Recently we played in Lapland as well as Italy. In two weeks we have a gig in Holland, then two in Istanbul and another one in Holland. Tomorrow, we drive to Berlin, that means another whole day traveling. We always go by train. My bass is in the luggage rack, that's no problem. The body on the one side and the neck on the other. I cannot sleep on the train, unfortunately. If I doze, I wake up with a stiff neck. The moving around takes a lot more energy than the playing itself. Chet plays best if we stay in one place for a while. Then he settles down, doesn't forget to eat, and his chops are all right. Besides everything else, he has problems with his denture. His gums shrink, there's less hold, and there's only one brand of denture cream that works for him. Recently Diane bought two big tubes of the stuff in the States because he always forgets. When he has to make do with another brand his playing falls off drastically."

It gets later and later, and Rocky suggests that I interview *him* instead. "After all," he say, "I have nothing to do; I don't know anyone in the city."

He tells me that his given name is Joachim and that he was born in Germany. As a child he moved to Canada, but came back fifteen years earlier to study contrabass at a conservatory. He is now 36 and tours with various American musicians.

"Since 1979 I work with Chet regularly. I accept all this shit because it is a challenge to work with him. His solos are always different, and there are only few musicians you can say that about. Many musicians seem original, but if you go on tour with them you find that they repeat themselves constantly.

"The absence of a drummer is very hard for me. Especially in a situation like yesterday evening. The whole time I heard that pop noise from the other room. Bass sounds in another key and another tempo. Just try and not let a super-slow ballad get even slower. Problems with the sound engineering? We have them everywhere. First of all, the technicians normally have no clue about jazz. And they don't understand how quietly Chet plays.

"The advantage of playing softly is that we can practice anywhere. Yesterday, we sat up here and practiced the whole day, twelve hours long, without a single complaint from the neighbors. The week before, we were in a hotel, Nicola Stilo got out his guitar, and we tried out new pieces. The other guests told me later that they turned off their radios and opened their windows in order to be able to hear better. No one is bothered by these sweet sounds."

Rocky remembers with some irritation the live recordings that they made for Rudolf Kreis' Circle label.* "The man just had to do everything by himself: the recording, production, the album covers—it was a one-man show.

*Round Midnight (Circle Records RK 23581/25); My Funny Valentine (Circle Records RK 23581/24); I Remember You (Circle Records RK 23581/28)

He ran around pompously, brought in a whole slew of microphones, but then he forgot to put one in front of the piano. I said, 'Shouldn't there be a mike at the piano?' No, he said, that wasn't necessary. The consequence is that you can't hear the piano on the records.

"I put up with all this, all these tiring tours, in order to remain a musician. For a time I did studio work, but that is deadly. You lose your interest in music and your musicality. I met a pianist recently who I hadn't seen in ten years. The whole period he had been playing 'schlagers,' German hits, which is about the worst music you can imagine. Now, he couldn't play at all anymore! He played all sorts of weird chords, and it didn't swing an inch."

Then, it became high time for Rocky to see to a few business matters. He had to call Wim Wigt to get instructions for the next concerts, 'because Chet always forgets'. Also, seats must be reserved for the train ride to Berlin the next day.

Meanwhile, it is 6:30—it has become evening. I have already spent half the day drinking coffee in the empty, semi-dark bar, and I find that it is now time to call it a day. My plans have turned into nothing, but at least I can say I've tried.

Two weeks later, the telephone rings. "Hello Jeroen, Tom here. Tom Mandersloot. Chet is sitting here beside me. He's staying here and tomorrow evening drives to Paris. From there he takes the plane to Istanbul. In the afternoon he has to be at the embassy for a little while to apply for a visa, and then he has a couple of hours free for an interview. Can you do it around 2:30?" He reas-

With Diane.
© Jacky Lepage

sures me: "I've told him who you are, and he was pleased. No, he'll come, I'll make sure of it. I'll be there too, just in case."

At the arranged time, I climb with Tom the typical-of-Amsterdam, extremely narrow stairway that leads to the floor where Chet lives. It is one big mess; the walls need a coat of paint. "We've haven't lived here long," Tom says, by way of apology. We speak briefly with Diane. After a short discussion we decide that the conversation will take place downstairs in De Stip.

After forty minutes of waiting Chet comes down. He is youthfully and fashionably dressed, in a bright blue jacket and a T-shirt with large lettering. Diane accompanies him. "Do you mind if I join you?", she asks. I make an inviting gesture and tell her not to hesitate if she has something to add to the discussion. In the course of the conversation she only says a few words.

I tell Chet that I was in the audience at the concert two weeks earlier in De Kroeg. "A difficult night," Chet says. "I had trouble with my chops. And I had to contend with a big herpes blister on my lip. If you look now, you can still see it. Then it was much bigger."

Chet is very polite and reserved and waits for each question. In contrast to other Americans he doesn't immediately serve up a whole string of anecdotes. The word *nice* is used repeatedly. His voice is deep, hoarse, and a little weary.

"The day after tomorrow, we play in Istanbul. Two gigs. We take the airplane from Paris. In a few hours, we are going to board the train."

Since 1975 you've been on tour continually. Don't you intend to settle down somewhere?

"Well, actually, we're in the process of looking for a place now. We're thinking about Amsterdam. I won't be home much, I keep going a lot anyway. But . . . Amsterdam is a beautiful city. Not too big, not too removed from my work. Right now I work mostly in Europe. Ninety percent of the time. Sometimes I go to Japan, and very occasionally I play in New York. Sometimes, I have a week or ten days free. But otherwise . . . working, travelling all the time."

That must be awfully exhausting.

(Shrugging) "Well, yes, it can be tiring when you're doing one-nighters. You play until late at night and then you have to get up early again to catch the train. You arrive, eat something, it gets to be time for the concert, you go to bed, and then have to get up again early . . . You know, on and on. It's a vicious circle."

You work with a select group of rather young European musicians—musicians from Italy, France, Belgium, Holland, and Germany, mostly. What are your criteria for choosing your sidemen?

"I choose them on the basis of . . . ahh, their musicality, their proficiency, and I also pay attention to their personality. Because you know you're going to spend a lot of time with somebody. It is important that you get along together, even outside the music."

I spoke recently with Evert Hekkema, John Engels, and Rocky Knauer. They are all relaxed types.

"Yes . . . Rocky is very laid back. Sometimes a little too much. He has a tendency to slow the tempo down. We often play without drummers, and that is very hard for a bass player. Because you don't have anyone else to support you. You have to set the time. And a feeling for tempo—either you have it or you don't. Bass players who don't have the time fixed in their head need a drummer to lean on. They need the hi-hat—tschick, tschick, tschick, tschick. The hi-hat on the two and the four.

"Ricardo Del Fra is an outstanding bass player if you want to play without a drummer. Because his time is

In concert with
Ricardo Del Fra.
© Jacky Lepage

very well fixed. So he doesn't need the support of a drummer. Jean-Louis [Rassinfosse] is also a good bass player, but his timing is not as strong as that of Ricardo. I always look for bass players who play precisely on the beat, with a good attack and a sound that resounds up to the next attack. [Sings] *Ding-ding-ding-ding-ding-ding-ding*. It often depends on the instrument. Some guys have a bass that produces only a little plop. [Sighs] Good bassists cost a lot of money and are hard to find."

You only rarely play with a drummer. Leo Mitchell, John Engels, maybe a couple of others.

"Yeah . . . I took John to Japan. In New York, though, I mostly play with a drummer. What the people expect there is a rhythm section with piano, bass, and drums. But I want to try it once without a drummer there too, because it affects the whole mood. The music becomes a lot quieter. I don't have to play so loudly in order to be heard. You know, cymbals ringing all the time. I like to play as softly as possible. The drums bring the volume up. Drummers are often too emphatic."

I recently saw that a dreadful album by you, Albert's House *[Chet lets out a shriek], is in the stores again. It amazes me that they have brought out this album again in particular. Don't they have any contact with you?*

"No. They never contact me. A part of the problem, of course, is that they don't know where I am. But they don't look very hard either, it seems to me. Barclay, Eddie Barclay, has brought out three of my records again: *Chet Baker in Paris, Volume 1 and 2* and a big-band record with Pierre Michelot.* I made these records in 1956, and since 1956 I haven't gotten a penny for them. And I often work in Paris. It shouldn't be all that hard for him to find me there. [Reflects briefly] 1956. That's a long time, eh?

"When I make a record now, I only get an advance. Some money in advance against royalties. And later I get to hear that that not enough records were sold to pay me royalties. Now, that's got to be bullshit. But I'll get a lawyer. I'll get them to open their books, in order to find out how many records they've actually sold."

Who's they?

"All the labels. Steeplechase, Timeless, all of them. Just tell me, why do they keep inviting me? If they earn so

---

*Chet Baker in Paris, *Vol. 1, 2, and 3 (Barclay Blue Star 80704 / 80705 / 8071); the last-named album is not a big-band recording little from me, why do they ask me over and over again?"

The album Albert's House *was made in a difficult period, no? Around 1969?*

"Yes . . . It was done at the time that I had all my teeth pulled. I had lost all my front teeth in an accident. I had to learn to play the trumpet all over again. I lived with my mother, I had a job at a gas station . . . It is a record with pieces by this comedian, what's his name again?"

Diane: "Steve Allen?"

Chet: "Yeah, Steve. He wrote most of the pieces on the record. That was 1970, I believe."

Diane: "No, that was before I met you."

Chet: "Maybe 1969."

There is another record on which you seem to have no desire to play. With the vibraphonist . . .

[Together] "Oh yeah, Lackerschmid."*

No, with Fred Raulston.

Diane: "Oh, that one? Have they brought that out? No one told us about that one."

Chet: "Which one?"

Diane: "Fred Raulston. The vibraphonist from . . .

---

*I actually had two albums in mind: *Ballads for Two* (Sandra SMP 2102) and *Baker/Lackerschmid* (Sandra SMP 2110)

Denver, I believe. No, not Denver, somewhere else. A vibraphonist from the States."

Chet: "Oh, yeah?"

Martha Burks is also on the record.

Chet: "Is she a singer? I can barely remember the whole thing."

Diane: "What's the record called?"

"Would You Believe."*

Chet: "Never heard of it. I never knew it was released. At least the other companies still release good records. *Mister B.*, on Timeless, with Michel and Ricardo, and the records with Philip Catherine and, ahhh . . . a bass player."†

What is the secret of your sound? Nobody else in the world has such a mellow, flugelhorn-like sound.

"That's hard to explain. The sound originated when I looked for a new embouchure. A way of playing for somebody who has no teeth. Look (*taps his front teeth*), these are dentures. Normally, when somebody loses his front teeth, particularly the front teeth of his upper jaw, that's it. You can't play any longer. But I worked hard at it. I managed to get a sound from my trumpet again, and I practiced some more to get the sound that I

---

*Fred Raulston Quartet, *Would You Believe* (Jazz Mark-103)

†*Mr. B.* (Timeless CDSJP 192); the bassist is Rassinfosse. The records with Catherine and Rassinfosse are: *Baker/Catherine/Rassinfosse* (Igloo OGL 0034); *Strollin'* (Enja 5005), and *Chet's Choice* (Criss Cross 1016 CD).

envisioned. I worked three years on it. Actually, it's no secret. I played a lot, and I had a clear idea about the way I wanted to sound."

You have a clear sound also in the low register. Other trumpeters sound a little muddy in the depths.

"I like to play in the deep register. I was never a high-note specialist. My range goes from the bottom of the horn up to around C or D. High D is about it for me. [He thinks briefly, moves the valves of an imaginary trumpet.] About two-and-a-half octaves, I think. But in these two-and-a-half octaves, I can say everything I have to say."

Does that have much to do with breath control?

"Yeah, controlling the airstream is very important. To be in a position to play long phrases, without having to gasp for air. You can only do it if you concentrate, so that you get the maximum out of the air that you blow into the trumpet."

The period that you played with Mulligan is described over and over as your best. I myself have the impression that you have done your best records since your comeback in 1974. Are you of the same opinion?

"Since 1974 I've played much better than in the '50s. I'm thinking of records like *You Can't Go Home Again*, *Baby Breeze*—do you know the record?—on the Limelight label. And, uhh, *Broken Wing*, with Phil Markowitz on piano. That's a beautiful record. With Jeff Brillinger on drums and a bassist . . . François

Kenny Clarke or someone like that. A French bassist. Good bassist.*

"They're nice, these records with Mulligan. There's no doubt about it. We created a new sound that was popular with a broad public. But the records after 1974 have greater value, much more depth. I play much better because I have all these years of experience behind me. In 1952, '53, I was another novice. I only played since 1947—jazz, that is. Now I've played jazz for forty years."

The stories about your break with Mulligan seem to contradict each other. Sometimes we hear he paid too little, other times that he was too overbearing.

"Well, he was the leader of course. He wrote the arrangements; he selected most of our repertoire, but one cannot say that he discovered me, as is sometimes claimed. Before I began to work with him, I had already played with Stan Getz and Charlie Parker. He called me once for a rehearsal, and then the pianist didn't show. So we played without a piano, and we noticed that we didn't need a piano at all. That was how the pianoless Gerry Mulligan Quartet got started. But it wasn't the case that he 'discovered' me, that he heard me playing and said, 'Yeah, I like that.' "

Did you leave the group because he didn't want to pay enough?

You Can't Go Home Again (A&M CD 0805 and 396997-2); *Baby Breeze* (EmArcy LS 86003); *Broken Wing* (Cornelia /ADDA 581020). *Baby Breeze* dates from 1964–65, before Chet's comeback. The bassist is Jean-François Jenny-Clark.

"Yes, that's right. I worked one year for him, for 125 dollars a week. At the end of that period I won all the polls. I was declared the best trumpeter in the world. And he won all the polls as baritone saxophonist. I went to Gerry and said, 'Gerry, it is all the same to me where we play, festivals, concerts, clubs, whatever, just give me 300 bucks a week. I've just been named the best trumpeter in the world. And he just laughed! He laughed in my face. As if I asked something completely ridiculous. So I called Russ Freeman and went on tour with my own quartet."

It seems as if Mulligan was not able to handle your success.

"Well, in that sense he is quite a bit of a . . . what's the word . . . "

Diane: "Prima donna."

"A prima donna. He wanted to be the star. It made him nervous if I got more applause than him. That disturbed him. It's the same with Stan Getz. I did a tour with Stan Getz about three years ago. We were supposed to give 32 concerts. After the seventeenth he called Wim Wigt to say that he didn't want to play another note with me. That he would immediately return to New York, if Wim didn't throw me out of the band. He found that he was getting too little attention. Very strange. Do I play tenor saxophone? I'm no threat to him. It's nonsense."

I have read somewhere that your father was a fan of Jack Teagarden. Has Teagarden influenced you? He also had a very mellow sound and a melodic style of playing.

"Well, I . . . I have certainly heard Jack Teagarden.
But not very often. I don't believe that he has really
influenced me. The biggest influences to which I
was exposed came from Miles Davis, umm, Dizzy, Art
Farmer, Kenny Dorham, Clifford Brown . . . Yeah, those
were my favorites. But I knew that I would only be successful when I developed my own style. Not if I tried to
sound exactly like Miles, Clifford, Dizzy, or whoever. I
had to find my own style. That is a laborious process."

*Don't you find that the great personalities of jazz are
practically extinct? Do you have the impression that you
belong with Stan Getz to the last of the Mohicans?*

"I guess so. We have lost so many. Zoot, Joe Farrell,
Sonny Criss, Sonny Stitt, Thelonious, Bud, Shelly
Manne, Philly Joe Jones, Paul Chambers . . . I can't
tell the young trumpeters apart. They all play like
Freddie Hubbard or Woody Shaw. They sound all alike,
as if they all come from Berklee. [Thoughtfully] But
there will always be something new, some other way
of doing it. I don't believe that jazz will ever really die.
It's a nice way to express yourself. It has supported me
for the last forty years, playing the trumpet. I've done
just that. I've never played in a big band. Well, once in
a while, in the studio.

"Recently a film was made, a documentary about my
life. I made the entire soundtrack with my group. I
think the film will be about an hour long. They interviewed my kids, Diane, everyone possible that I've met
in the music business, Russ Freeman . . . I think it will

be a nice film. It will premiere at the next film festival in Cannes."*

Is it true that you're self-taught? In your repertoire are pieces with complicated harmonies, "Conception," for example . . .

"Well, I can't read chord sequences. I can play a melody line that is written down for trumpet. But chord symbols tell me nothing. If we play a new piece, and it doesn't have the usual AABA form—if it is unusual in one way or another—I have to hear it a few times before I can play a solo. My father gave me a trumpet, and I tried to get a sound out of it; that's how it started. For a time I went to instrument training class in junior high school. That was the only instruction that I ever had. Blowing long notes, scales, and a little sight reading."

Do you still travel to the States now and then in order to visit your children?

"I saw them recently, six weeks ago. Yes." [There is silence for a time. Chet doesn't give the impression that he wants to talk about the subject.]

Did you play there, in the States?

"No . . . I don't play there much. But every time I play in New York, it's a packed house. The fans are still there and still show up when I appear somewhere."

---

*Let's Get Lost lasts two hours and premiered at the Venice Film Festival in 1988. The soundtrack is Chet Baker Sings and Plays from the Film Let's Get Lost (RCA Novus 3054-2-N).

And can they appreciate your music? Don't they expect a trumpeter to play loud and high?

"No, they don't expect that of me."

Have you done records recently?

"O, I am very active, as usual. In a short time the soundtrack to the film will come out, and I have just done two records for the Japanese market. One is called *Singing in the Midnight*, the other *Love Song.** Did you know about them? Wim Wigt will bring them out, so they will be available in Europe sooner or later. There was one year that I made fourteen records. [Chet probably means 1979, when he took part in at least eleven recording sessions.] I also did a record with Wolfgang Lackerschmid again recently. Only vibra-phone, trumpet, and bass. And a little synthesizer, here and there."

You've said that you would like to live in Amsterdam. Do you already have a house in mind?

"We might rent the top floor above De Stip. From Tom. We're still discussing that at the moment. It has to be polished up a little. It is a nice big room. I'm thinking of maybe giving workshops there. We've already talked it over with someone from Muziekpakhuis [a music school in Amsterdam]."

**Singing in the Midnight* (Polydor KK J33J 20153) and *Love Song* (RVC/Baystate R32J-1065)—both CD. Reissued by Timeless as *Cool Cat* (SJP 262) and *As Time Goes By* (SJP 251/ 252)

That's better than living in hotels, in any case.

"Yes."

I cannot understand how someone who is nearly sixty can put up with constantly travelling the world, from Paris to Istanbul, from New York to the North Pole.

Diane [whispering]: "It's difficult." Chet [drily]: "That's life."

Chet gets up and says that it's getting time to go to the embassy in order to pick up the passports. If the necessary stamps are in it, Chet and Diane, according to plan, can take the train to Paris the same evening, then board the train to Istanbul. Doesn't Chet have to pack? "I don't have much luggage," he says, "and my trumpet is already packed."

Before he goes, we talk a little more. Chet is full of praise for John Engels. "That's really a drummer with good timing. He's a natural." About *Albert's House*: "The accompaniment sounded like an organ with a rhythm machine." About *Would You Believe*: "I played maybe one good solo, the rest was just air and spit."

I stick around another hour with Tom. Just as I leave De Stip, Chet and Diane come running. From a distance, they could be mistaken for a young couple. "Bye, Jerome," Chet says, and waves.

on tour: evert hekkema and wim wigt productions

*W*im Wigt: "Since 1983 I've organized nearly all of Chet's concerts. It began with a tour with Stan Getz. I wanted to have Chet as a guest in Getz's group. The tour took place in February 1983. I brought both of them to Europe.

"Well, from the beginning the two didn't get along very well. I met Stan in New York at the end of 1982, and he said, 'Chet came by last night at Fat Tuesday's and he looked like a bum. I have no desire to go on tour with a guy like that. I've been a junkie, I freed myself from that world, and I don't want to have people like that around me any more. He asked for money and he looked like a bum. Take Chet or me—or cancel the whole tour.'

"Now, I had already given Stan an advance. Chet also, but not as much; he wasn't used to getting such sums yet. He was happy as a child with the 500 bucks I gave him. So we settled the matter, more or less, and even completed 17 concerts. Chet continually played the stars out of the sky, and Getz wasn't too happy about it. It's

something Getz is always struggling with. He has a
gigantic inferiority complex, for which there is no reason
at all. He made like he was cool, but all along . . . He was
also constantly asked, like: Why are you touring with
such a person? You shouldn't do that! Now, Getz is very
suggestible. He is open to every insinuation. Chet was as
high as the sky, every day, but he had more success than
Getz. And Getz, he simply couldn't get in shape to blow.
He was down every day, and couldn't muster the energy
any longer. After the seventeenth concert, Getz said:
'Him or me.' At that time, Getz was the bigger name.
With him the tour could still proceed in good order. So I

*With Stan Getz
at Montmarte,
Copenhagen,
1983.*
© Jan Persson

decided in favor of Getz, but I paid Chet for the remaining concerts anyway.

"Chet gave me a lot of credit for this gesture. It wasn't something he was used to—getting paid for eleven concerts that he didn't play. At his request, I had to open an individual account for this money—the only time that Chet had any money in the bank! After two months, it was spent. Chet wasn't accustomed, yet, to having so much money in the bag. *(Laughs)* Later, of course, he was. Before, he had lousy jobs in small clubs. But not long after, his fee was twice and sometimes three times as much.

"The only reason the tour lasted as long as it did was that the Sonet label had contracted with Getz to do a recording session. They wanted Getz and Chet together on the record. So Getz had to wait before bringing down the axe. They wanted to release a radio broadcast in Stockholm and so they made a deal with Getz.* He was the leader, so far as they were concerned, and so he got the money: 17,000 dollars. Of that, he only gave Chet 2,000. That's Mr. Getz for you. Immediately after the concert in Stockholm, the tour was broken off. I was very angry over it. I thought Getz had no class.

"Chet stayed in Europe afterward, and I arranged appearances for him. They became more and more frequent. We started with 500 dollars. By the time he died, his minimum was a thousand. Cash on the spot. Chet intended to increase it to at least 1,500 dollars and play

*Baker/Getz: The Stockholm Concerts (Verve 537 55-2)

fewer concerts. At the end he was getting $5,000 for each record.

"In the first year, he was completely unreliable. He did-n't show up for half the gigs. In commercial terms, a can-cellation rate of 50%. Little by little, things got better. Because I got used to him. I took his habits into account. I learned that you always had to give him ample time to get somewhere. I learned to factor in the ups and downs of his frame of mind.

"You have to picture it like a curve—a curve with valleys during the times when he used too much and spun out of control. Then he would fly to America to relax, and after a few months would return. At the time he died, he was in one of the valleys again. He was about to spin out, and I expected he would shortly leave for the States again. Actually, he was not happy in the States. But he always went there when he was stressed out.

"Over there, he had virtually disappeared from the scene. In the winter, he could stay with friends in California, or with his mother in Oklahoma. He could not get drugs as easily there. He had a reputation in the States that dis-couraged people from hiring him. Once a year he played New York, and occasionally he had an engagement in LA, but he missed half of them. He would arrive a day late, or not show at all. When he was back in Europe he rarely spoke of his visit to the States. He once mentioned that he had been to see his kids. In general he never referred to Carol. Actually, he rarely spoke of his family to any extent.

"Between concerts, he often stayed in Amsterdam. For a

time he lived with Evert; later he lodged with Tom and Linda Mandersloot. Sometimes in a hotel. He was often in Luik with Jacques Pelzer, as well, and then he would drive to Amsterdam for a day or two. Completely unpredictable, quite irregular."

Evert Hekkema plays trumpet and baritone sax. Chet and Diane regularly lived in a room that Evert and the author of this book had cleaned and painted completely white for him. Evert met him on May 14, 1983 in an Amsterdam hotel. Until 1986, Chet had a key for Evert's apartment in Amsterdam Oud-West, on the second floor of a house at the Da Costakade.

In Denmark,

1978.

© Jørgen Bo

Evert Hekkema: "One day the telephone rang, and to my great surprise it was Chet Baker. He was looking for a car and had heard from pianist Irv Rochlin that I wanted to unload mine cheap. A little while later I drove with the car to the Crest hotel in Buitenveldert where he lived. He took it for a spin around the hotel to see how he liked it, and then we agreed on a price. The car was not insured, but that didn't bother him.

"Later, while we were drinking a beer at the hotel bar, I told him that when we were young we used to admire his album covers, and would style our hair just like his. Once he had his hair combed backwards with brilliantine, another time he had a real short bebop haircut, and we copied it exactly. He was a true teen idol. Chet was moved to hear that. 'It never occurred to me that on the other side of the ocean people tried to act like me.' When he went to get cigarettes, his friend Diane said, 'Can't you go with him to one of the weed shops? At least then he'll stay in a good mood.' I said, 'I happen to have some on me, so that won't be necessary.' So we went to his room and smoked a little there while the TV ran. All of a sudden a little man came on the screen, a politician from a very right-wing party, spouting all sorts of racist slogans. 'What's he saying?', Chet wanted to know. I translated, and he said, 'Oh, that reminds me of last night in the train.'

"Chet told me that he and his sidemen had come by train from Paris. They settled themselves in the first-class cabin, where a very respectable-looking American couple were sitting already. Chet was dressed all in black, and on his slight head he wore a black hat with a red band.

They put the instruments—contrabass, percussion, trumpet cases—into the luggage rack and sat down. The American looked at him suspiciously and asked: 'Do you have a first-class ticket?' Chet answered evasively, 'We'll see about that.' After a long silence, the American whispers behind his hand to his wife, 'I can't stand that smell.' But Chet has very good hearing. He immediately gets up and flings the window open wide. So now the couple is sitting in the airstream, with their gray hair blowing all around. After he has recovered a little of his nerve, the man says, 'Could you please close the window?' Chet announces: 'This window stays open until the smell is completely gone.' Again silence. The American gathers all his courage and says, 'We would like to have a pleasant trip.' Chet replies, 'Listen, asshole, if you fuck with me you will have the most unpleasant trip you ever had in your life.' The rest of the train ride they sat opposite each other, without exchanging another word, both too proud to move to another compartment. The trip lasted eight-and-a-half hours."

Evert remembers that Chet once flew over from Scandinavia for a day. He had taken the plane just to buy something in Amsterdam. Before he went to his connection, he stopped by Evert's house to drop off a shopping bag. He opened the door, woke Evert up—it was still early for a jazz musician—and pushed the bag under Evert's pillows with the message: "Just look after this for a while." The bag seemed to contain a rather large number of bills from all over Europe. Evert started to count them and arrived at a sum of about 15,000 dollars.

Wim Wigt: "I don't believe there is anyone who has spent

so much money on drugs in one lifetime. The Six Million Dollar Man. He sometimes seemed to be proud of it. Most addicts spend less money and die earlier."

Peter Huijts: "Others would have died with his way of life long ago. He was a tough guy. He was also quite strong. We got into an argument once and wound up wrestling on the ground. After that I also noticed that whenever he gave you a poke in fun, it could hurt quite a bit."

Evert and Chet sometimes played duets. Evert played a solo, Chet blew a bass line, and the roles were then exchanged. Chet was taken with the musical abilities of his host and in October 1983 invited him on a three-week tour of Italy. The other musicians were Michel Graillier, Ricardo Del Fra, and Leo Mitchell.

Evert Hekkema: "It was hard work. We did twenty appearances in three weeks, and sometimes we had to put 350 miles behind us in a day. We drove by minibus through the country. Michel and I alternated at the wheel, Chet and Diane made themselves comfortable on a mattress.

"We were always punctual, always at the venue the usual three-quarters of an hour ahead of time. We arrived late only once, and that was the grandest gig of the whole tour. In the conservatory of Turin, an enormous domed hall. We reached the city on time, but Chet still had to buy something, and finally we were an hour late.

"A whole crowd of men were sitting in tuxedos, and ladies in evening gowns. The Italian manager who had organized the concert was there too, completely stressed out. He was furious at us. He wouldn't talk to Chet. Chet said laconically, 'Don't worry, we'll tell him that a headlight broke.' 'I think that's rather a lame excuse,' I said. 'It's good enough,' Chet answered casually.

"An hour after the official beginning of the concert, Chet finally came on the stage. He wore a red sweater and bath slippers, and he hadn't cut his toenails in at least a month. He sat down and started in with 'Beatrice,' a piece by Sam Rivers. After the first note an ovation broke out; everyone was so glad he was finally playing. And the trumpet sounded so fantastic in that gigantic space."

Harry Emmery: "Chet rarely came late when I worked with him. Yes, sometimes there were problems with his denture. Then, we simply couldn't start. Once, in Switzerland, he was nowhere to be found—not in the hotel, and certainly not in the hall. But a quarter-hour before the concert was to start he came walking in with his case, completely relaxed. Once he started, he played long sets. He didn't want to stop. The managers of the club weren't too enthusiastic about that. In many clubs, nothing could be served as long as you played. Chet played two hours at a time. Then a waiter would ask me to tell Chet that it was high time for a break."

The Italian pianist and arranger Mike Melillo made a tour with Chet and an Italian symphony orchestra in July 1985. To the irritation of the orchestra, Chet didn't come to the rehearsals. The orchestra musicians had no experience of jazz, and considered it completely outrageous that the soloist didn't attend the rehearsals. The evening of the first concert, he was still nowhere to be seen an hour before showtime. So Melillo could forget about a general rehearsal as well. Only a few minutes before the start, Chet reported to Melillo with the assurance that everything would go well on the tour, with our without rehearsals, because: "I can't read music too well—I play by ear." Melillo remembers that the concerts proceeded perfectly even if Chet sometimes appeared only ten minutes before the start and occasionally even a half-hour late (*Musica Jazz*, July 1988).

Almost all the musicians who worked with Chet in the '80s speak with admiration of Peter Huijts, Wim Wigt's tour manager. The success of Chet's recordings and overseas tours in the last five years of his life is owed in no small part to Huijts' efforts.

Peter Huijts: "It's my job to see that things proceed as smoothly as possible. To try and get the musicians on the stage on time, and shield them a little from outside influences. With Chet, that also meant seeing that he ate and slept regularly. When he had no desire to go eat anywhere, I had to think of getting something for him. Oh, he could eat like a wolf. But if he was on heroin, then it was a hamburger and a milkshake and that was it.

"Wim had to take care of the sidemen mostly. I still remember a tour with a quartet through Scandinavia, not long before his death. We had not relayed the names of the musicians to the organizers, because they changed on occasion. We spent whole evenings ringing up pianists and bassists. We knew who Chet liked to play with and we tried to get these people. But what he wanted was not always feasible—we cannot have an American pianist flown in for one gig in Vienna. When we went to Japan in 1987, Chet had almost loaded in a big band. He had asked all friends, 'Are you coming with us to Japan?' That wouldn't work, of course. We had to intervene.

"One of the strangest associations was with Archie Shepp in March 1988.* Those were weird concerts. Two completely different musicians who had never played together before. At the start, it was very stressful. Chet needs space. He would play a phrase, wait a few bars and then resume. While Archie blew non-stop. If Chet just paused for a moment, Archie immediately came in with a big surge of sound. And then Chet sat there with an expression as if to say, 'Fine, go ahead, if it's so important to you.' At the second concert in Paris, I talked with Shepp about it. 'This is how Chet is,' I said. 'If you go on like this, we won't get much music out of him.' That evening things went a little better.

"Once, he was supposed to give a concert in the Concordia Theater in Enschede, Holland. It was due to begin about 8:15, but he hadn't shown. Luckily he had been considerate enough to call ahead and say he would be a little late. So I told the organizers, he's going to come late, but he's going to come. But then it got later and later. At 10:00 he was still not there. The management of the theater came to me and said, Let's cancel the thing, it's not going to happen. I said, Let's wait till 10:30. If he's not here by then, then it's over, everyone

*They can be heard together on *In Memory Of* (Bellaphon LR 45006).

167

gets their money back. At 10:28 he came with his car at a high speed. I said, 'Goddam it, Chet, you have to be on stage by 10:30, or the concert's called off.' He unpacked his trumpet and ran on stage. Well, the first half-hour he got barely a note out of his trumpet. He still had to get his denture in place; his embouchure was completely lacking. He sat quietly in his corner. But—and this was not the first time I experienced it—he persevered until things improved. It just got gradually better. And, to the frustration of the theater management, he played until one in the morning. After that he even went to De Tor, the club next door, where he continued to play with Jacques Pelzer until four."

Ria Wigt: "Chet was supposed to play in Nancy, France, once, with Michel Graillier. From our office we phoned his hotel in Paris every half hour to make sure he left in time, and Michel did the same thing from Nancy. The whole day we asked him, 'Where are you? Are you leaving in time? When are you leaving?', and so forth. All at once, he wasn't there. He was supposed to return to the hotel to call us back, but we never heard from him. At nine o'clock Michel said, 'Chet is not in Paris, and he is not here either, so let's forget it. He's not in shape to play for other reasons, anyway, so I'll start without him.' I said: 'No, Michel, you have to keep trying.' Michel was annoyed—he was dead tired and had drunk too much. But we pooled our resources and called every conceivable person. Finally we gave up. The next day, we heard to our astonishment that Chet had arrived in Nancy about one that night and played the stars out of the sky. I took part in such adventures countless times.

"Once, he had to go from Rome to another city. Well, how much effort that cost me . . . I had to mobilize half of Rome to get Chet out of the hotel on time, and get his bill paid. I sent a telex and called the airport with a request: 'There is an older man heading your way who is not very coherent at the moment, but he must depart without delay, please can you help me?' When he got off the airplane, we had to arrange a taxi—and all this from our tiny office in Wageningen.

"There, I was busy the whole day with it, calling everyone possible, most of whom I didn't know, to say: 'The tickets, which he forgot, are lying ready at that hotel room, and they must be sent at once to that place . . .'

"Once he showed up at a rehearsal two days late. We had to talk and talk and be extremely kind with the orchestra and the organizers to make it all up. He was often in a bad mood for days, would insult us over the telephone. That was really unpleasant. When he spoke again, we'd say, 'Chet, what do you want? Do you want to stop playing altogether? We can't carry on like this.' But, no, then he would be especially eager to play. He always attracted trouble. Take the beginning of the Japanese tour. When the plane took off, it turned out that he was still in Rome. So he had to get another visa . . .

"Once we had arranged a ticket for him to fly from New York to Europe. I drove to Paris to pick him up. But there it turned out he had flown to Montreal to play there with Paul Bley. A disastrous concert. He fell in with the wrong people there and fell asleep on stage. Two days later we managed to talk to him. But now he's in New York without any money. He calls to ask whether we could send money for a new ticket. Which was pretty difficult since he didn't have an account and the weekend had just begun.

"In 1987 we had a concert in Verona. There, he had forgotten his trumpet. He had intended to drive from Italy to visit Pelzer because he had something to do there or because he had some ridiculously small gig or other scheduled, and it wasn't until he reached Munich that it hit him: Damn, I forgot my trumpet. And instead of going back to fetch it he went on to Luik, and then thought: Now what? Or maybe he didn't think at all. In the meantime we had called God and the whole world in order to find him. And then we hired assistants to make sure that he got onto the plane in Brussels on time. And arrange for a trumpet. He arrived in Verona, and then we had him flown to Milan in a private plane hastily rented for the occasion. And when we had managed all that, we learn that the gig was cancelled because it was raining and the concert was supposed to be held outdoors."

Under the watchful eyes of Peter Huijts Chet was an especially pleasant colleague and traveling companion. The Dutch drummer John Engels toured twice—in 1986 and 1987—through Japan with him. Chet was taking only methadone then, and the tours proceeded smoothly. For Engels, the tour represented a teenage dream come true. "I became a professional musician in the early '50s, when I was 17, and there were a few musicians I wanted to play with: Tommy Flanagan, Flip Philips, Hank Jones . . . and Chet Baker. The first record I bought was by Chet Baker. An EP—*Chet Plays*

Compositions by Russ Freeman—with, among other things, 'Bea's Flat.' Now I've done it—it's happened. I've played with all of them. The Japanese tours were the climax of my career. First I thought, It will be a mess. I had seen Chet at a concert in De Stip. He sat on a barstool and stared straight ahead of him. It was like looking at a corpse. At one point, a valve on his trumpet got stuck, and he tried to loosen it by pouring Coke over it. Well, that of course made it worse. And then he unloosened the valve and right away a small feather jumped out, which he then started searching for on the floor—what a drama.

"But on the tours, everything ran smoothly. That's because Wim Wigt had sent along a guy whose job was to look after Chet: Peter Huijts. The guy should have got a medal. I have a video of a concert in Tokyo here.* Chet wore a good suit and played simply divinely. I believe he would still play in a good suit and look like a young god if Peter had stayed with him. Chet played fantastic. I can state that objectively, because I recorded several concerts. Altogether some 35 hours of music. Every concert was more beautiful than the last. The record doesn't actually capture him at his best.† When Chet died, I could not put the tapes on for months. It was too much for me. I've heard plenty of funny stories of course, but I only had good experiences with Chet. If he had gone out of control in Japan, it would have been a shock.

---

*The music from the concert is available as *Memories* (King Records / Paddle Wheel K32Y) and *Four* (King Records / Paddle Wheel K32Y 6281); most recent issue: *Live in Tokyo* (Evidence ECD 22158-2).

† Engels refers to *Sings Again* (Timeless CDSJP 238).

Something would have shattered in me. He was just an awfully nice human being. Yeah, Chet . . . We didn't speak that much together, but we understood each other. We communicated through the music."

Peter Huijts: "In Japan he took nothing, only methadone. His whole personality changed as a result. He became quite a friendly guy, who played much better, much more powerfully. But if you talked to him, he didn't seem too happy about it. I said to him, 'Do you see that you can do it—go three weeks without taking anything?' He said, 'Yeah, sure, but I don't get a kick from methadone.' Methadone gives a mild high and prevents withdrawal symptoms. It kept him from being sick. But he didn't feel good with it.

"His tone really developed in Japan. In Europe, you never knew how he was going to play. Of course, he could also play well on heroin. I had the impression that that he was all right if he could regularly get hold of methadone as well as heroin. He could dole them out very shrewdly. But if he went any length of time completely without, then things deteriorated. When he got back to Amsterdam from Italy or Sweden, for instance, where he could hardly score at all, then he would take so much that he could barely play a note for several days. There was no heroin there, while there was plenty here, so he would completely flip out. If the laws had been somewhat laxer, we would have had less disastrous concerts . . . "

Wim Wigt: "Chet went to Amsterdam because of the favorable heroin prices, but also to get methadone from a house doctor that he knew well, a 'Doctor Bob.' In order to ease his conscience he would get some methadone, and would even tell himself that he was going to stop, which of course he never did."

Evert Hekkema: "A few months later he lost the car that I sold him in the neighborhood. It turned out that he had left the house keys in the car along with the car key. So he walked back to my house. It was around midnight, and I wasn't home. Chet had no wish to run back and look for the car again, because he had drunk a few whisky sodas, and they hadn't gone down well. It seemed to him to be the best solution to climb up, along the balconies at the rear. He knew that the kitchen door above stood open. So he rang below, asking politely whether he could just be allowed to go through the house, to the garden. Well, he had luck there, because a middle-aged couple lived there, and the woman had been listening to Chet Baker records since the '50s. She had also seen a recent photo of him and knew for sure that this was him. Her husband didn't believe a word of it. He only wanted to go to bed, and then a bedraggled form rings, claiming to be Chet Baker.

"Finally, though, they let him into the garden. He said that they should have no worries because he had once served with the army in a commando unit. He climbed up like a cat, Diane later told me, and even brought a T-shirt with him that had fallen off my clothesline above.

"One day, Chet walked to the toilet. He stopped in front of a mirror in the hall and recited: 'Mirror, mirror on the wall, who is the fairest of them all?' He was silent for a while studying his features. 'Not you, motherfucker,' he answered himself, and kept walking."

in deepest
concentration:
in the studio

*f*rom 1977 on, Chet played on a large number of records as leader or co-leader. At the time of writing, more than 100 of them have been released. They appeared mainly on small labels like Wim Wigt's Timeless, on Criss Cross (Holland), Steeplechase (Denmark), Sonet (Sweden), Philology (Italy) and Circle, Enja, and Sandra (Germany). The owner of Criss Cross is Gerrie Teekens. In September 1984, he organized a recording session for Chet in collaboration with tenor saxophonist Warne Marsh.*

Gerrie Teekens: "Marsh was in Holland for a tour, and it struck me as an intriguing combination. So I called Chet, who also thought it was a good idea. He said he had always admired the guys from the Tristano movement because they were such honest musicians—Marsh especially. They didn't genuflect before the almighty dollar. It seemed quite natural for Marsh to work with Chet—who was straight, clean and sober. The negotiations went smoothly. I arranged with him by telephone:

*Blues for a Reason (Criss Cross 1010)

'Next Sunday at six o'clock in the evening in Max Bolleman's studio in Monster, near The Hague.' Chet said, 'All right, I'll be there.'

"But later, I began to have doubts. Everything had gone a little too quickly for me. I wanted to call him one more time before this Sunday to confirm everything. I finally managed to reach him in Paris. I got a woman on the line, probably his friend Diane. Chet was sleeping. I introduced myself and explained why I was calling. Then she asked me, What time is it?' 'Four o'clock,' I said. 'Daytime or nighttime?' she asked. You see, that's how these people lived. They no longer knew whether it was day or night. Later, Chet came to the telephone. 'Don't worry,' he said. 'If I say I'll come, then I'll be there.'

"On the day of the session, Chet arrived by car from Rome. He had driven the distance in one shot. About a quarter before six, he was in the studio. That shows how well he knew the European highways. He retired for a brief time to fight his tiredness with a few medications and then we got going. I let Chet decide for the most part what he wanted to play. I always do that in the studio. Now and then, I'd make a suggestion, like: 'What do you think of a blues?', or 'Isn't it time we did a ballad, or an up-tempo number?' Like that. Just to furnish some variety. And I didn't like to have bossa numbers. For a jazz album one should stick to the jazz repertoire. But that was no problem for Chet.

"I had suggested on the phone that he might play a few pieces with a mute. Chet said, 'I'd like to try that too, but I don't have one.' So I said, 'I'll get one for you.' So I set

Italy, 1979.

© Carlo Verri

about finding a mute, and Chet used it. No problem. Around 1:30 in the morning, we were ready. Warne was very pleased with the session. Chet was considering whether he should drive through directly to Paris with Micheline Pelzer, who had attended the session, or whether he should make a side-trip to Evert's house in Amsterdam, to rest a little. But he drove with Micheline to Paris. He sat down in the car again, and later I heard that he covered the whole distance again at the wheel, without a break.

"In June of the same year I had him enter the studio with the guitarist Philip Catherine for the first session of *Chet's Choice*. I invited Hein Van de Geyn to play bass. I had heard so many good things about him. And Hein plays acoustic bass. Jean-Louis Rassinfosse, who formed a regular trio with Chet and Catherine, always played on a 'Van Zalinge bass,' this electronic contrabass without body. I didn't like that.

"But Chet had difficulties with his denture. His denture cream just wouldn't hold. When it finally did set, it was still a while before his chops were there. He played a lot with the mute in order to hide his problems. He tried singing on a couple of numbers, but his voice was shaky, and we had to repeat it. What we ultimately got on tape wasn't bad, but I was a little disappointed.

"Two weeks later, he played at a jazz festival in Münster. This concert incidentally was also recorded.* Münster is not far from Enschede, where I live, so I went. I spoke with him in the dressing room and asked him how the session went. 'Oh, pretty well,' he muttered without much conviction. 'I know that it could have been better,' I said. 'Well, fine, let's do it over,' he suggested. I said, 'What's that going to cost me? I don't have an unlimited budget.' 'It'll cost you nothing at all,' he said. I thought that was a fantastic gesture on the part of someone who went through money so quickly.

"At the second session, a few days later, he came by car from Paris again directly, but he was in top form. The

*Strollin' (Enja 5005)

second session went from nine o'clock at night until about one. It went quickly. For each piece, we did one, at most two takes. To make sure that he would show up rested and well fed in the studio I went with him and Diane to a Chinese restaurant. We gossiped a little about old and mutual friends in the States. That was a good idea. Chet has the tendency to neglect himself. Later I combined a small part of the first session with most of the second, and that became *Chet's Choice*.

"Since then we've stayed in constant contact. When I was in New York for recording sessions we went out together to eat. He complained about sometimes needing money in America. Well, I lent him some, but always got it back. For as long as I knew him Chet was never late, was always friendly, and dependable in commercial matters. Later I brought out another record with a radio transfer from Nick Vollebregt's Jazz Café with pianist Phil Markowitz. That also went off without problems. I called Chet, and he agreed. He thought a lot of Markowitz. We agreed on a sum, and in a few minutes, the matter was settled."

In 1983 Chet recorded eight records in Max Bolleman's Studio 44 in the small town of Monster at The Hague. Bolleman: "The sessions were very uneven. Once it didn't go at all, another time it ran like a dream. Sometimes, he came much too late or not at all. Sometimes he was sick and sat there and just howled. There were sessions that resulted in barely a note of music. It really wasn't simple. I often had to adopt the role of producer as well. But if he had a good day, it went well. A record like *Mister B.* we did in seven hours [Timeless CDSJP 192].

A night's work, and that was it.

"In December 1986, Chet recorded the music for two CDs in a day and a half.* He was flown in special from the US to my studio. I'm very proud of it. The Japanese producers who got the idea, thought, 'Just let Bolleman take care of it—he knows how to handle Chet.' Someone like Rudy van Gelder doesn't have the patience. No time to fool around, just play. I'm the opposite. I don't look at the clock even if it becomes night work. I'm also a musician, I play drums—I know what it's like. You have to make sure the musicians feel good, that they have as much time as they need to make something decent out of it.

"During the session Chet sat in a recording booth by himself, otherwise I would not have gotten him on the tape well. The man played so incredibly quietly. And the singing that is whispering . . . I made it as comfortable for him as I could. One microphone for the singing and another one a little lower for the trumpet. In the sound booth he felt right at home. He sat there quite comfortably with his denture cream, his ice-cream—he liked ice-cream—and a headphone, which allowed him to listen to himself. As you know, in the last years before his death he was on the lookout for an apartment. After the recording he asked me: 'Can I live in this booth? How much do you charge for rent?'

"When a session proceeded so well, you had to leave him

*Singing in the Midnight (KK J33J-20153 CD); and Love Song (RVC/Baystate R32J 1065 CD) alone in silence as long as you could. After each take he would sit there quietly for three or four minutes. Hunched over, his head between his knees. No one was allowed to disturb him then. At first I thought—the man has fallen asleep. But he was reflecting back on the recording; he let everything affect him. After a few minutes, the judgment came down in his sad whisper: Do it over, or not. Once I said, 'I don't think you quite hit the chord in this or that bar.' Chet whispered, 'You don't have to tell me when I'm wrong.' So I never said anything like that again. Chet was such a pro, you didn't have to tell him anything.

"The hard work came later. When Chet sings, there are all possible interferences. On many tracks I had to splice dozens of segments to get rid of all the clicks from his denture. Enormous work."

Gerrie Teekens: "The problem was also that Chet didn't always play close to the microphone. He sometimes leaned way back, while other times he blasted full-strength directly into the mike. Later, Max would have to adjust the volume of the trumpet solo until it was in good balance with the other instruments. If you listen closely, you can hear that in some places Max has to make Chet louder."

Max Bolleman: "Once he was all mixed up. Then he told me to build my kit, because he wanted to drum. Of course, that made no sense considering the expensive studio hours. Ricardo Del Fra said: 'Keep calm, let him have his own way, then he'll calm down a little.' Ricardo remained quite friendly under these circumstances. A very capable man.

"Chet made a very tender, vulnerable impression, but he could make people do whatever he wanted. He had quite a refined manner to influence you. Oh, I took part in some things . . . At three o'clock in the morning I had to wake up the pharmacist to get this special denture sticking-stuff. The pharmacist didn't open. We rampaged until he opened finally. My wife Els had to go into the city in the middle of the night for hash . . . There's no limit to the things one did for him."

Wim Wigt: "Usually he was at his best in the studio. He concentrated the most then. But after that he didn't care about the production or the selection of takes. He left to others what got published. Still, he only made a few bad records. Yeah, the series for Circle.* No one could do anything about it. Sometimes he needed money, and then no one could prevent him from anything. He simply did whatever he wanted. If for instance he went two or three weeks without giving a concert, then his money would be gone, and he'd accept any gig. He didn't look after his rights. Not when he was younger either. Just look at all these reissues, which he didn't get a penny for. He would just sign, he never paid attention to the contract conditions. 'Who cares!' Well, not then anyway. Later it dawned on him. Then, other people were to blame. He saw the records in the stores and used to gripe that all the labels were cheating him."

*Night Bird (RK 25680/23; My Funny Valentine (RK 25681/24); Round Midnight (RK 25681/25); In Your Own Sweet Way (RK 22380/26); Just Friends (RK 22380/27); I Remember You (RK 23581/28); Conception (RK 27680/32); and Down (RK 22380/35)—all LP

Peter Huijts: "Chet always wanted to be independent, actually, to run his own business, manage, but it was beyond him. And every time it became clear that he couldn't actually work without somebody to manage the concerts for him and organize the recording sessions, he'd get really pissed. Then he'd think: 'I'm being cheated.' A lot of musicians of his generation think that way."

Wim Wigt: "Whenever somebody offered him a contract, then everything was forgotten again, then he just wanted to earn some quick money. *Who cares!* His family, his estate—he never looked after them. He would always say, 'I'm trying to get as much as I can now, because I don't have too many years to go.' Chet is now, after his death, more famous than ever. His records sold well then, they sell even better now. Actually, I should have recorded him more often. But there was enough trouble with Chet already. I didn't have too much time and energy left."

who cares? chet baker's last year, and his legacy

*I*n the last months of his life, Chet was very active. He frequently went on tour, and while in Europe his recording activity was undiminished. When I met him in September 1987, he had just completed a successful tour of Japan with Harold Danko, Hein Van de Geyn, and John Engels. In the first half of 1987 he spent some time in the US for (among other things) the filming of *Let's Get Lost*.

Let's Get Lost, a dramatized documentary in black & white, lasts 119 minutes and is directed by Bruce Weber, a famous fashion photographer. The film incorporates segments from the film *Hell's Horizon* (1955), in which the young Chet has a small role, an appearance on the Steve Allen Show, and a concert with the festival of San Remo in 1956. Chet, his mother, Carol Baker, and their children all appear in the film, as do Diane, Ruth Young, Jack Sheldon, and Dick Bock (who died one year after the filming at the age of 61). The actor Robert Wagner can be seen as an (overdubbed) trumpeter in a clip from the film *Fine Young Cannibals* (1960), in a part originally intended for Chet.

Let's Get Lost was much praised by film buffs, but harshly criticized in the jazz press—no wonder, since the soundtrack doesn't do Chet justice at all. He was only allowed to play slow pieces, songs that were mostly outside his repertoire. He had to sing on every number, and the recordings were made when his lips and vocal cords were in poor shape.

The film contains a lot of information about Chet Baker. Some interviews from the film—and the 'Film Journal,' a book containing photos and interviews—are quoted in this book. And yet the film and the publicity surrounding it were the source of not a few misconceptions. It was represented as a documentary of Chet's last year, which it was not; the shooting with Chet took place in the first half of 1987. The soundtrack, too—recorded in these same months—was said to be Chet's last recording. In reality, Chet's music after the second (and last) recording session for *Let's Gets Lost* is available on about 19 CDs, both live and studio sessions. On most of them, he plays much better than on the soundtrack.

The trumpet player is presented as a mumbling skeleton, barely able to play his instrument properly anymore and saved from oblivion by the director. According to the liner notes of the CD *Boston, 1954* (released in 1992), Weber 'selected Baker, now a lonely and mostly forgotten drug addict, to be the subject of a biographical documentary.' The photo collection *Young Chet* (1993)—a wonderful collection of William Claxton's work—also describes Chet as completely 'forgotten.' Rarely can someone 'forgotten' be enjoying so much acclaim.

At Montmartre,
Copenhagen,
1988.

© Jan Persson

After the release of Chet's Japanese recordings in the US in 1996,* attitudes gradually seemed to change. Noted author Francis Davis writes in the liner notes: "These two discs from Tokyo find Baker in peak form less than a year before his fatal fall from the window of an Amsterdam hotel room . . . The real surprise here is Baker's clean execution on fast tempos . . . Maybe he was never as inarticulate or 'limited' a soloist as he was usually portrayed."

Memories and *Four* were issued as the double CD *Chet Baker in Tokyo* (Evidence Music).

187

Let's Get Lost premiered in September 1988 in Venice, and received the Italian Critics' Prize. The film was also nominated for an Academy Award. That honor, however, went in April 1989 to a documentary about the war criminal Klaus Barbie.

In July 1987, Chet was back in Europe and back in harness: a long series of concerts for Wim Wigt, mainly in France, Germany, Italy, Scandinavia, and Holland, ensued. Early the following year, Wigt arranged for two guest appearances with the Archie Shepp quartet: on March 13, 1988 in the Frankfurt Congress Hall, and the following evening in the New Morning, a club in Paris where he often performed. He also arranged that their collaboration be recorded.*

The first concert was hardly a success. Just prior to the scheduled rehearsal, at noon in Frankfurt, Chet suddenly left for Italy to buy a new Alfa Romeo. The objections of Peter Huijts and the musicians could not deter him. He flew to Italy, bought the cream-colored car, and returned with it to Frankfurt the same day. The consequence was that he stood exhausted on the stage and hardly took part in the proceedings. The public—6000 in number—and the critics were not exactly enthusiastic. In order to prevent repetition of a similar situation, Huijts swapped his airline ticket for Chet's car keys. The following day in Paris he played somewhat better.

Such incidents indicate that Chet during this time was losing control over himself again. His drug use was becom-

*Released as *In Memory Of* (Bellaphon L & R 45006)

ing extreme, and—what's worse—in March, Diane left him and returned to the US. It is not clear what the immediate occasion for her departure was—a small dispute could have sufficed to break off their difficult relationship. Chet would never see her again. On April 15, the trumpeter was present at a concert of the Italian tenorist Gianni Basso in the Milanese club Al Capolinea. Chet was in a good mood and returned the next evening to sit in with Basso's group. They agreed to meet up in Belgium in the middle of May. On April 17, Chet, with his Alfa Romeo, drove from Milan to the German town of Rosenheim. The concert was recorded, and released after Chet's death as *Last Recordings as Quartet.** Chet sounds good, but the recording quality leaves a lot to be desired. The following day, he gave 'a very decent concert' (Wim Wigt's description) in Brunswick. On April 28 followed a concert with the big band and symphony orchestra of North German Radio. Chet played excellently. The concert was released on Enja as *My Favourite Songs* and *Straight from the Heart.*[†]

On April 30 Chet got money from Wim Wigt for the last time. The performance that evening was in Calais, and Wigt gave him in cash, besides the $2500 for the concert, $4000 as part of his payment for the album with Archie Shepp. Wigt: "In Calais Chet gave his last good concert. Afterward he was so oppressed by drugs that things really didn't go any more."

**Live In Rosenheim—Last Recordings As Quartet* (Timeless 233)

[†] *Chet Baker My Favorite Songs—The Last Great Concert Vol 1* (Enja 5097);
Chet Baker Straight From The Heart—The Last Great Concert Vol 2 (Enja 6020)

Chet played in the Parisian New Morning again on May 5. The concert was well attended. The proprietor of the club, Egal Fahri, told Mike Zwerin in an interview for *Wire*: "We always did good business with Chet. I think one reason is that people thought each time might be the last." For a couple of numbers he was joined by German pianist Joachim Kühn. Kühn in *Wire*: "He seemed very tired. It was so sad. I remember thinking that this can't go on much longer" (*The Wire*, July 1988).

Two days later, on May 7, he concertized at the Thelonious in Rotterdam. There were only a few people in the club, and Chet was in no condition. He needs a fix. He cannot locate his car fast enough after the concert and travels instead by night train to Amsterdam. Wigt: "Chet got paid nothing or almost nothing. Willem van Empel [manager of this jazz center at the time] thought that Chet played so bad that he didn't have to pay him anything. Besides, attendance had been so poor that there was hardly any gate."

Chet spent the night of May 9–10 in the Capitol hotel on the Nieuwe Zijds Voorburgwal in Amsterdam. On Tuesday, May 10th he called the bass player Harry Emmery about a concert scheduled for the following week. According to Emmery, there was nothing out of the ordinary about Chet or his phone call. He simply had a gig and matter-of-factly asked if Harry was available. On the same day, Chet drove back to Rotterdam to get his car, the cream Alfa Romeo with the Italian license plates. In the afternoon, Wigt got a telephone call from Chet from a Rotterdam police station.

At Montmartre,
Copenhagen,
1988.

© Jan Persson

Wim Wigt: "I got a scare. I immediately thought: I have to get there right away. It turned out later that my fear was justified, because I heard that his shoes were full of drugs. But as it turned out, it was no big deal, he was only at the station because he wanted to report that his car was missing. He was not well. He needed a roof over his head, and someone had to be there to look after him until the concert two days later when he was supposed to play with Archie Shepp in Laren. And his car was missing. I needed someone who was a little familiar with the surroundings of the Thelonious in Rotterdam. So I hit upon Bob Holland [nickname of Robert van der Feyst]. Bob had worked for me earlier. He lived in Rotterdam and also had trumpeter Woody Shaw and tenor saxophonist Frank Wright staying with him—so maybe Chet could join them. I called Bob Holland asking him to help Chet out of the jam. Although he didn't know Chet personally, he agreed. He picked him up from the police station Haagse Veer."

Van der Feyst at the time lodged several drug-addicted musicians, for whom he also organized concerts. The trumpeter Woody Shaw, who lived with him several months, would die May 10, 1989, nearly a year to the day after Chet's death.

Van der Feyst brought Chet to his house. Chet took a shot and ate (a little) with Van der Feyst and Wright. Woody Shaw had just left the country. Around midnight Chet let it be known that he wanted to play. The group made their way to the jazz club Dizzy, also in Rotterdam. That evening they had Bad Circuits, a jazz-rock band of young Dutch musicians: Jasper Blom (tenor), Rob van Bavel (piano), Boudewijn Lucas (bass), and Hans Eykenaar (drums). Chet sat in on two pieces of the concert's last set, which ended around one. Van der Feyst reported later that he played 'with a strength and intensity that I had never heard from him before' (*Vrij Nederland*, May 21, 1988). The saxophonist of the group was less charitable: "Chet Baker didn't have his best day obviously; he looked bad, and his ideas only came out haltingly. It testified to some vigor that he took the initiative to play along, but apart from that he made a sorry impression. He entered with Bob Holland, just as we were playing a piece by Hans Eykenaar, 'R.C.'—an abbreviation for Rhythm Changes. The piece is based on 'I Got Rhythm,' but that gets a little obscured in the theme. The tenor solo proceeds over a pedal tone. But as soon as the piano solo begins, you can clearly hear what the chords are. And that's when Chet began to play along.

"We had to gallantly make allowances, but we managed. Of course, we played rather 'heavy.' We immediately brought the volume down; otherwise we never could have heard him. Next we played 'On Green Dolphin Street' with him. A couple of times he whispered in my ear that he could play a lot better, and that he was having trouble with his chops. His playing still had a certain charm. He could express his ideas concisely. But I think that only for someone who had heard a lot of jazz was it clear what he wanted to express."

Afterward Chet joined Rotterdam's nightlife to find an establishment where he could purchase drugs. He was gone the whole night, and didn't return to Van der Feyst's apartment until early Wednesday morning. He then slept all the way through until Thursday morning. The police called Van der Feyst to report that Chet's car has been found. Around noon, Thursday, Van der Feyst headed out to get the car and at the same time some heroin for his guests. What happens next I have reported in the first chapter: Van der Feyst stays away too long for Chet's taste, and Chet decides to take the train to Amsterdam. That night, he is found around three o'clock behind the

Prins Hendrik hotel, dead on impact after a fall or jump from the window of his hotel room.

Criminal Inspector R. Bloos showed me some photos from Chet's file. Shortly after his death, his room looked as follows: To the left, on the bed (which had not been slept in—the bedspread was undisturbed) lay some clothing. To the right on the ground, an open trumpet case with his instrument and some papers. On the table, a remarkable amount of cocaine and heroin. Chet (who had already taken some) probably intended to have another speedball—heroin and cocaine in combination. (*In Let's Get Lost* he says this was his favorite high.)

Before that could happen, however, he had fallen from the window or had jumped. He landed on the narrow sidewalk, between the stone posts and the hotel. He was wearing a pair of striped pants, was barefoot and had his sleeves rolled up. The police followed the usual procedure. Around the spot where he landed, a red-and-white-striped tape was stretched; the body was covered with a white sheet and removed on a stretcher.

R. Bloos' suspicions go strongly in the direction of 'LSD-type conditions': "Hallucinations and so forth. I have dealt with such cases already. People who went for a stroll on the rain gutter . . . The pants marks in the dust on the sill showed that Chet had sat there some time, then straightened up and fell downward." Although Bruce Weber never made the effort to acquaint himself at first hand with the circumstances of Chet's death, he suggested in many interviews that Chet has been murdered, and that the police had handled the case carelessly

—remarks that were snatched up greedily by journalists at the time. Since his death a strange but persistent rumor has been in circulation—that Chet had been thrown out of his hotel after a dispute, tried to climb the façade of the hotel, and fell in the process. Criminal Inspector Bloos: "Nonsense. First of all there was no mention of a dispute, in conversations with either the guests or the hotel personnel. Moreover, any child can see that it would be impossible to climb the front of that hotel even a meter. And even if he had managed to do that, he would not have landed on his head but on the lower part of his body."

The police report contains a precise account of Chet's possessions at the time of his death. In the room, they found the sum of 59.90 guilders (about $30), a cheap lighter and a pearl necklace—besides the drugs. There was also his watch—a Citizen Quartz—and the trumpet. This instrument—a Vincent Bach Stradivarius—was not his property, but was on loan from the French Selmer factory. The Alfa Romeo was parked outside. All these objects—except the car—were turned over to Peter Huijts on May 13th.

Wigt has calculated that Chet in 1983 earned three to four thousand dollars per month, while in his two last years he made approximately $25,000 a month. Chet's death was for Archie Shepp immediate cause to demand higher royalties since his record with Chet was now more valuable.

Peter Huijts: "His death touched me very deeply. I blamed myself, thinking like: If I had only responded to certain signs better . . . I had just gotten back from a three-week tour with Dizzy and was completely worn out. I didn't know what had happened in the meantime. Chet was in a difficult period again as I learned later. So I came back exhausted from the tour with Dizzy and called him on May 12th about one at Bob Holland's in Rotterdam, to arrange with him when and where a co-worker of Wim would pick him up that evening in Amsterdam. Chet was in a lousy mood. He was furious. 'Fuck you,' and so forth. You never knew why—and I never asked. A little later I called him again and managed to make him understand that he would be picked up about seven in the Memphis Hotel, where rooms had been reserved for the musicians. I thought: 'Let's call it a day, I need some sleep.' I would certainly have needed two hours to get from my apartment in Eibergen to Rotterdam, and Chet could not have waited that long.

"At the start of the concert, I was not especially concerned. He had failed to appear before. For the duration of the concert I was merely annoyed. But later in the evening I began to worry. Because in general you would hear from him. Usually he would call in the course of the evening, with some story or other about something that hadn't happened and why he hadn't come. He always had an excuse, a flat tire or something. But now there was nothing.

"I don't believe he wanted to kill himself. He was weakened, stoned, and then such things can happen. He needed company that night. I myself would help him sometimes when Diane wasn't there. I would bring him to his room, and say: 'Good night, Chet, we're going to bed.' Then he would say, 'You can sleep here.' Sometimes he would stay up all night running up and down, stamping around, overturning everything, completely mixed up because he couldn't get something. I accompanied his body on the trip to California for the funeral. It was my way of saying goodbye —a way of taking leave. I needed that for myself."

Chet was buried amid minimal public sympathy beside his father in the Inglewood Cemetery outside of Los Angeles. Chet's mother had bought a little spot of earth there a long time earlier. The burial was organized and paid for by Bruce Weber. Although he undertook all that, the director and Chet's family are no longer on good terms.

Weber: "When Chet died we helped bring his body over to the US—his family didn't do anything. We paid for his funeral and organized the whole thing; we'd spent so much time with this man that we had grown to feel very strongly about him. And his family never said thank you to anybody on the crew . . . As they left the funeral they turned and gave the production lady the finger—that's the way they said thank you . . .

"I think they thought that because they were Chet Baker's family that they could get away with certain things in life. Chet was never interested in that side of life—he was never a man to be tied down—and his whole family obviously resented that . . . They certainly resented the relationship we had. They hated every one of the film crew, it was like, 'What are you gonna do for us?' But the movie isn't about them, it's about Chet Baker—he's the only one who matters" (*The Face*, November 1988).

Carol Baker: "It's true that Weber paid for the burial. But nobody can accuse me of anything. I had no money. The insurance wouldn't give the money because the circumstances of Chet's death were so strange."

Wim Wigt: "One should not judge Carol too harshly. I've talked to her about it. You see, at first she simply didn't have the money, even if she had wanted to. She has always had only modest jobs and she had to support her children as well, who still hung around at home, because they were not very ambitious; Chet often groused about it when he was back here. She had been married to him for about 25 years when he died. In the last ten years she had a husband who used up all the money himself. He had done nothing to bring up the children. As far as I know, he never gave Carol and the children any money. She had to do take care of everything. The insurance refused to pay. And Carol thought that the whole burial was a Bruce Weber Production. She believed that he wanted to use the opportunity to take a few sentimental pictures. So she thought, Good, take them and pay for the whole thing while you're at it."

Chet's death is only briefly noted at the end of *Let's Get Lost*. Weber did not alter the film after Chet's death.

Wim Wigt: "He hardly ever spoke of 'later.' About what would happen after his death. And he never talked about his family. Yes, once he said, 'I hope you'll remember me when I'm gone.' He wanted people to remember him. But he did not do that for his relatives, one shouldn't have any illusions about that. Peter [Huijts] indeed tried to talk to him about making a will. But Peter had to choose an appropriate moment to do it, and that was certainly not so simple, and then Chet was not attentive long enough to really arrange matters. 'Who cares?' "

"as though it were his last time...": a lyric trumpeter

*t*echnically speaking, Chet should not have become a trumpeter at all. When he had been playing trumpet for half a year, he was struck by a rock that knocked out his left front tooth. Limits were immediately set to his technique. He hardly practiced and took no lessons, if one discounts some group instruction in Junior High School. In *Let's Get Lost* Jack Sheldon speaks with envy of the young Chet, who played fantastic trumpet without ever practicing: "Sound, phrasing, it all came naturally."

Evert Hekkema: "I never once saw him practice, he wouldn't even warm up before a concert. In that sense, he was downright lazy. When he went on tour, he gradually got into shape, simply because he performed regularly. But otherwise he did nothing about it."

Peter Huijts: "Once in a great while, if he was in a good mood, he would want to rehearse. Then, the band would meet at noon. If Nicola Stilo was around, he played the guitar. But there was nothing like a regular rehearsal schedule."

In bad times, Chet didn't make the effort to take care of

himself. Then he often appeared dirty, unshaven, and run down. His trumpet was just as little looked after. Evert Hekkema: "I looked into his trumpet once. Well, it was full of dirt, and there was only a small hole for the air to pass through. I immediately set to cleaning the instrument. It was unbelievable, a ball of green dirt the size of a child's fist came out. It surprised me that he could still play on so dirty an instrument. Chet said, seemingly anxious, 'Oh, I hope that cleaning won't affect my mellow sound.' But he didn't mean that seriously, he was smiling that shy smile."

The trumpet is a physically demanding instrument, but Chet (to say the least) neglected his health. As early as 1955 he had to contend with tooth decay in an advanced state. He told journalists at the time that he expected it would end his playing. He had bad teeth to begin with, and took scant care of them. The tooth decay was exacerbated by a poor physical constitution as a consequence of an irregular life, bad nutrition, and drugs.

It was probably tooth problems, then, that in the period 1963–1968 induced him to switch to flugelhorn. This instrument is not suitable for long escapades in the high register and is hard to keep in tune, but without too much effort can generate a nice sound in the middle range. In 1966, after he had already played approximately a quarter century without the left upper incisor, Chet lost a part of the other front tooth as well. About two years later, he finally had all his teeth pulled and began wearing a denture.

According to Chet, it was a catastrophe: colleagues

In Toronto,

Canada, mid-'70s.

© Paul J. Hoeffler

apparently told him it would be impossible to play trumpet with dentures. But was it really as bad as all that? In the opinion of most trumpeters whom I have spoken with, it is not an insurmountable problem. One learns to play trumpet today without exerting pressure on the lip: the non-pressure method. In practice, it is true, the trumpeter must press a little if wants to play high and loud. In that case the upper incisors act as support.

Woody Shaw managed to play without his upper teeth during about the last five years of his life. The trumpeter Edu Ninck Blok, who has followed Chet's career closely and played with him several times—including 1985, when Chet made a record with the Amstel Octet under Ninck Blok's direction—was able to name right off another trumpeter with an artificial denture: Bunk Johnson (1889–1949).

"And I have a record on which he plays trumpet very well with it, musically and technically. When you lose your teeth, you have to retrain your embouchure, but you can still do a lot. Of course, you can't be a lead trumpeter any more; you need an outstanding set of teeth for that. But if you are content with the middle register, you can still play for years. Even before his comeback, Chet rarely went higher than a high C or maybe D. He had no need to play that high.

"He had a good embouchure. Right out of the book: he squeezed the corners of his mouth together and formed a kind of pillow for the mouthpiece to rest on. He didn't press too much, because then the lips are no longer well supplied with blood. The less strength one uses, the less one presses, the deeper and more beautiful the sound that results."

Ack van Rooyen knows of no trumpeter with a complete set of artificial teeth, but is certain that Maynard Ferguson has a bridge for his upper incisors. "The problem is that you have to learn to play all over again. If the new teeth are even a fraction of an inch differently positioned, it makes a huge difference. And the relationship between the upper and lower jaw changes. Ideally, you press the mouthpiece evenly against the upper and lower jaw. Every trumpeter, in fact, should have a mold of his teeth done, in case something happens to them. Then the doctors can recreate them as close to the originals as possible. But not every one thinks of such things."

Van Rooyen agrees with Ninck Block: In the high register a denture is a handicap, but can be no problem in the middle register. In sum, the denture problem seems to be less formidable than Chet believed. The transition cost him a good deal of work for two or three years. For the first time since his youth he had to practice for hours. And he never cared for that in the first place. Usually, if he unpacked his trumpet in a hotel room or at a friend's house, it was at best only to jam a little. Never to blow long notes or scales. But now he had to overcome his aversion and go through purely technical exercises.

When Chet got the mouthpiece, he lost the few high notes he had. To compensate, he went even lower than before, because he could obviously manage that without too much pressure. He gradually turned into a low-register specialist.

Evert Hekkema: "In the low end, he had incredibly clear articulation. That is very difficult, not only because you have to depress so many valves—in the high register you can play almost anything with two valves—but because you have to relax your lips completely. Even in fast passages Chet's lines could be followed note for note. He played about a half octave lower than the average jazz trumpeter.

"He really needed a microphone then. The deep notes are more difficult to hear, especially when you play so softly. And he could be really venomous if the amplification people didn't do their job right. Yeah, he whispered on the trumpet. It amazed me that he could produce so clear a sound even at such low volume. It has to do with concentration and breath control. He refused to be rushed, and took time to mold every note. If his chops weren't there, he would sing. He told me that once. That way he gave his lips a rest. A long piano solo, a bass solo, a little scat...that's how he survived. Yes, Chet was very clever. He was so experienced—he knew exactly what his limitations were.

"You could say that his style following his comeback was the product of an embouchure that limited his playing in a technical sense, his restricted harmonic knowledge— and great resourcefulness to overcome both."

Chet once said: "My dream horn would be one that I didn't have to blow in, that I could just press the valves and the music would come out." After his comeback he preferred to play sitting down, with a microphone and a monitor (a part of the p.a. system that allows musicians to hear their own playing) within reach. Yet, despite his supposed 'laziness,' he didn't always make it easy for himself.

Evert Hekkema: "I remember that he always gave his best, really. He always played as though it were his last time, and he mostly looked as if he would never play again. There are many trumpeters who play things that come easy to the instrument when improvising. Chet was different. He mainly thought melodically. And if it called for something difficult, technically speaking, then so be it. You can have a lot of success with a few simple tricks. Half-pressed valves, or a trill with the third valve. Lee Morgan—who could play fantastic trumpet, of course—often did that. In Chet's solos, you never hear such effects.

"He always liked to play trumpet slumped in a chair. He let his elbows rest on his knees, so the trumpet didn't become too heavy for him. Of course, it didn't look too good. But Chet liked it. He longer had to prove anything. It would never to occur to *me* to give a concert like that. Once in a great while he got it in his mind to show off. Then he would stand up, step back a ways from the microphone and blast away, high and loud, like Fats Navarro. If I had played a good solo, he didn't want to lag behind. Of course, he had no 'high,' but he knew how to position the few high notes he had in such a way that he seemed to be blowing very high. He made each note crystal clear and his intonation was more precise than anyone's. You were forced to listen as a result. You thought, Pay attention—this is important."

Chet played different trumpets. With wonderful regularity, his trumpets were 'stolen'—which usually meant that he pawned or had lost them—and then he had to get hold of another. In 1954 he appeared as the principal actor in an ad for Martin trumpets. He told *Jazz Hot* that he played a Martin, the Committee model, for 'a very long time.' The flugelhorn he played in the mid-'60s was a fine French Selmer. After his comeback he switched to a Conn Constellation. Chet found the instrument expen-

sive and clumsy—in the sense that it was quite heavy—and not very tractable at the high end. But its dark tone in the low and middle register pleased him very much.

After one Conn was 'stolen' in New York—probably in 1982—he found an affordable student model—a Buescher. "It plays in tune without having to do a lot of work and lipping up and down" (*The Wire*, November 1983). When Chet appeared in Norway in August 1983 for a tour with pianist Per Husby, his trumpet had supposedly been stolen in Paris. He played a series of concerts on borrowed instruments, and afterward reacquired the same cheap Buescher model. In 1986 he switched from the Buescher to a Getzen Capri, and in the final year and a half before his death he played on a trumpet that the Selmer Company had lent him.

Edu Ninck Blok: "After his comeback Chet nearly always played on mediocre instruments. He would rather spend money on drugs and hotels than on a better instrument. And that, even at a time when he was earning a lot. Once, he did a Scandinavian tour for Wigt with twenty concerts. He earned 40,000 guilders [about $20,000] in one month for it. With it he bought methadone from 'Dr. Bob'—he was the jazz doctor who always prescribed methadone for him. But after a few concerts, he had enough of the methadone, he got no kick from it, so he hopped in a taxi and took the first flight to Amsterdam to score. He got his fix, and flew right back. Yes, the money certainly went fast . . .

At Cinema Teatro

Anteo, Milan,

Italy, November

1979.

"In the '50s he played on a Martin. That was a good choice. Almost all the best trumpeters of his generation played on a Martin—Miles Davis, Clark Terry, Kenny Dorham, Lee Morgan, and many others. It is a trumpet that is quiet, but has a full, warm sound.

"In later years Chet paid more attention to whether the valves were easy to work than to any other qualities of a trumpet. He was a real virtuoso on the valves. He moved his fingers very economically, that's how he could play so quickly. For years he had the Buescher. In 1986, I saw him in the Bimhuis with a Getzen Capri, a mid-level instrument. He thought, I can get my mellow sound out of any trumpet. But in reality he deserved a better trumpet. Because his sound, that was three-quarters due to him and one-quarter from the trumpet. Only a year and a half before he died did he start to play a first-class instrument again—a Vincent Bach Stradivarius. Peter Huijts had arranged for that with the Selmer Co. in France.

"Something I thought was very clever: He consistently played on a mouthpiece with the same caliber. Only during his flugelhorn period did that change. His lips got used to the edge of the mouthpiece. In the '50s he had a 6-B mouthpiece—which is rather deep—and after his comeback a 6-C. That is flatter, but the edge, the diameter, is identical. So he almost always played with the same caliber. Sometimes he would replace his horn, but keep the mouthpiece. A deep mouthpiece gives you a full, dark sound. I know only a few famous jazz trumpeters with a flat mouthpiece. Howard McGhee is the only one I can think of now. He had something like a 7-E."

Chet was an isolated phenomenon, one-of-a-kind. He

was no innovator, no trendsetter. During his successful years he was a model for some young trumpeters, but his influence was short-lived. In general, I don't think he was strongly influenced by anyone, either. There are two records on which he clearly tends to Miles Davis: *Chet in New York* and *Once Upon a Summertime* (OJCCD 207-2 and OJCCD OJC-405). Most of his other records feature playing that only occasionally betrays this or that trait in common with Miles: a dark tone, a spare, melodic approach. When asked about the trumpeters he admired, Chet would simply recite a list of a number of big trumpeters from his generation: Miles, Kenny Dorham, Fats Navarro, Clifford Brown, and Dizzy Gillespie. Except for Miles, he emulated none of them. At most one can speak of a certain similarity: it is evident, for instance, that Dorham, Farmer, and Chet all belong to the same generation—but that's all. He was of the opinion that the younger trumpeters invest their playing with little personality. Of Wynton Marsalis he said, "He has a lot of technique and no soul" (*Jazz Press*, September 17, 1975).

As a singer, too, Chet was completely his own man. In the interview with *Jazz Hot* he said that he liked to listen to Frank Sinatra, Tony Bennett, and Mel Tormé. Once again, he simply names a few good artists with whom he had grown up. No one of them, it seems to me, influenced him decisively.

In 1987 Astrud Gilberto said: "I learned about Chet through Joao Gilberto, when I was in my teens, and I became such a great admirer of Chet that subconsciously I may have absorbed some of his style." She was proud of the fact that she had once recorded a number with him.* "It had nothing to do with fame, just musical admiration" [from *Let's Get Lost*]. She has some things in common with Chet: a thin, light voice, an introverted manner, a refined sense of timing. Gilberto is a singer whose forte, in contrast to Sarah Vaughan, was not technique, but tunefulness and a compelling presentation of the lyric.

Lee Konitz: "I have always thought of Chet as a singer. However lousy his condition might be, he was always capable of singing, very lyrically and emotionally. Even when he had trouble with his lips, he could always produce pure musical notes with his voice. That quality kept him alive through all the years of drug problems."

Evert Hekkema: "Ah, the voice. Well, he sang quite directly, quite forcefully. His singing had a strength that captivated you, just like Billie Holiday. You can't just ignore him. You either have to listen to him, or turn him off."

Criticism is often leveled at the sidemen of his later years. Initially, Chet just played with the best young musicians who were available. Later, other factors came into play. Did the potential colleague use drugs, for example? Many were allowed to play along, as often as they wanted—Jacques Pelzer, for example—because they were indispensable for extra-musical reasons. But he continued to set the highest musical standards for his rhythm sections.

That girl from Ipanema (Rare Bird CD BID 1101)

On the Conn,
Canada, mid-'70s.
© Paul J. Hoeffler

Peter Huijts: "There were often problems with pianists. Chet needed a lot of room in his music to express himself. That's also why he played so seldom with drummers. He once said: 'They influence my feeling for space, they shut me in. They want to determine the direction of the music, they're too dominant. I can't do what I want to do.' Pianists who played too much drove him completely nuts. I won't name names. Sometimes it went along all right for a while, then he got fed up and immediately had to get a new one.

"On top of that, they hardly ever practiced. He simply went on stage with a few musicians and played a number. The others just had to follow him. The musicians had to know every tune in every key. He could be really mean, especially with young bassists and pianists who didn't know every piece by heart."

Harry Emmery: "He had high standards for bass players. We often played without a drummer. The best thing you could do was play simple and strong and not try anything fancy. Rhythm was the most important thing to him. As far as chords were concerned, you just had to follow him. He made it very clear when improvising which har-monies he wanted to hear. He was less demanding when it came to other horn players. He just let them play along—that annoyed me sometimes."

As improviser, Chet always remained true to himself. Even on the most commercial albums he played taste-fully and stuck to his style. He always wanted to please his audience, but cheap publicity effects were complete-ly alien to his playing. The accounts of colleagues and friends give a picture of the genuine improviser, who took unexpected detours again and again.

Peter Huijts: "It was so beautiful. Over and over this tor-ture with the instrument, and over and over again the music that was always distinct. Chet was one of the few musicians who play every evening differently. He had a repertoire of about thirty pieces that he was comfortable with, but he always played them differently. I was pres-ent as his tour manager at about 150 of his concerts, and every concert was a new adventure. With most musicians whom I've toured with, after a couple of evenings I've heard it all."

Evert Hekkema: "No matter how many bars he stopped

playing to think or take a breath, no matter how little he played, he always maintained the tempo. You could always hear where he was. For all his notorious antics, I never heard Chet play a wrong note, or lose the beat, or get confused in the course of a piece. He was so absolutely music that he didn't have to worry about it anymore."

After Chet's death, the Italian pianist Enrico Pieranunzi said in *Musica Jazz* that he was most impressed by Chet's deep concentration when making music, and by the fact that he never played clichés. A song remained alive even if Chet had played it dozen of times. "He always chose the piece on which he could express himself the best. A standard was for him like a human being, in which one always finds something new."

The trombonist Jimmy Knepper: "I knew him when he was a clean-cut young fellow in Los Angeles. He was a wonderful player. He didn't do anything spectacular, he just played music. Just good music. A lot of heart. That's my bag. If somebody plays that way, I love him." John Engels: "I sometimes hear it said, He makes mistakes, he can't sing, and so forth. I can get real annoyed. I think: Don't you have ears? Can't you hear that the man is telling a story? Whoever is creative falls flat on his face once in a while. The way someone goes into the unknown and finds his way out again, that can be fascinating. With him you never knew what was going to happen. Rehearse? Never. He began a number, and we followed him. We always played with 200% concentration. Because of him I begin to think differently about music, and play differently too. The cat played with an intensity that you only find among the true greats. Among Billie Holiday and Lester Young. He played with warmth and love. When it went well, I was the happiest human being in the world. It may sound sentimental, but Chet opened something up inside me. He went deeper than anyone else. And that's what it's all about, the intensity. Chet came from another star. He was sent here to convey his message. Now he's back on the star he came from."*

Mike Zwerin (the American-born author now living in France): "You do not generally feel like jumping up and shouting 'Yeah!' after a Chet Baker solo. All that tenderness, turmoil and pain has driven you too far inside. He reaches that same part of us as a late Beethoven string quartet, a spiritual hole where music becomes religion . . . To his fans, Baker becomes the measure by which to judge the honesty quotient in others. He goes for feeling first, with just as much technique as he needs. Other improvisers try and overwhelm the trumpet; blast it fast, screech down the walls of Jericho. Baker builds new walls. He needs them for protection. He always plays seated, folded in a question mark. Between solos, he sits, trumpet resting on his crossed legs, without moving. You almost say to yourself—my God, he's passed away up there. Then, ever so slowly, he raises the instrument to his lips and when those sweetly burned innocent notes bloom again it's a relief, almost as though you've made it through one more winter."[†]

---

*John Engels did some concerts and record dates with Chet in Europe and two lengthy tours in Japan in 1986 and 1987.

[†] *Close Enough For Jazz* (London/New York 1983)

quite a regular guy: colleagues and friends on chet baker the man

*L*ee Konitz: "As a touring artist you are constantly surrounded by people who want something from you. People ask you for everything imaginable, offer you things . . . Chet couldn't shut himself off, he was open to everything that happened around him.

"Yesterday, somebody came backstage and started insulting me. He thought I played badly and said so in a very unpleasant way. I said: 'This is the dressing room, what are you doing back here?' and told him to get lost. If you take drugs, you can't do that. At certain moments you get an enormous kick, but later you're even more susceptible to exactly those things you've escaped from. You don't even have control over yourself. You're always in the victim's role.

"I'm often in Europe on tour. On the stage, I have success, I communicate with the public. But when I leave the stage, I'm a mere mortal again, trying to get along in the world. No one knows me, only the jazz insiders, and I don't speak the languages. Everywhere there are people who try and cheat this 'Ugly American.' And I fight it:

'Hey, you're charging me too much, No, that's not right!'
I don't like to have to act that way, but I have the alternative of either doing it or being cheated.

"Chet let all this affect him and then would suddenly get in a horrible mood in a completely uncontrolled way. Once, we were supposed to rehearse in a music school where I taught. The principal, who sat behind a desk below, didn't know Chet and asked him what he was doing there. When Chet heard that he began to abuse the guy. And he wouldn't let up. I think I lost the job because of that incident. He looked like a tramp and was treated accordingly.

"Anytime someone wants to tell me a story about Chet Baker, I say, 'Stop, let it alone,' because I already know it's going to be a sad story. Chet got in trouble all the time."

Evert Hekkema: "Sometimes he had paranoid attacks. He had terrible fears that Diane was involved with someone else. He would also make scenes over money. Sometimes, he was very generous, and then again small sums could be occasions for big scenes. He never paid rent for the room in my house. But he paid 1500 guilders—half the price—for my baritone sax. He knew Diane a long time, since 1970 or so. For about nine years after that they did not see each other, and that disturbed him terribly. Because, who knows, maybe she was up to something with other men in the meantime."

Peter Huijts: "I never completely understood Diane. How can anyone stay together with a man for so long who causes so many problems? Who is practically asocial? And Chet was so jealous. Probably we have all such feelings, but if you're a junkie those fears are reinforced. To be sure, he realized that it was impossible to live forever with something like him. Then it was back and forth, she would regularly leave to visit her family in America."

Evert Hekkema: "During the day, when he went to find drugs, she had to stay in the hotel. And when he gave a concert, she also had to be with him so that he could keep an eye on her. If she was terribly tired, she was allowed to remain in the hotel in the evening, as an exception. But then he called during the break in order to make sure she was really in her room. Why did she remain with him so long? Love, admiration, solicitude. She found it difficult to give her life meaning.

"Yes, Chet . . . You put up with everything for him. When he lived with me he really caused some trouble with his drugs and his quarrels with Diane. If other people had behaved like that, I would have said to them immediately: 'Go to a hotel! Leave me alone!' "

Peter Huijts: "Diane was about ten years younger than Chet and played a little soprano saxophone. Chet always wanted her to play on stage, but she never dared. I think they needed each other. Diane found it hard to make decisions independently. Life with him certainly had its agreeable side. All the touring, you see many countries and get to know people. She was not such a strong personality. Well, why did all of us like Chet? If one wants to analyze that, one stands before a puzzle. I never got anything back from him. Only his music, in the evening, on stage. I once said to him, 'You can only communicate on the stage.' He looked at me with an acid smile through his small reading glasses and muttered something like: 'You've figured it out.' Deep conversations were just about impossible. When you talked with him it was usually superficial."

According to the Italian tenor saxophonist Gianni Basso, Chet 'died of loneliness' (*Musica Jazz*, July 1988). "He often shut himself up in his hotel room for days at a time. It was not very agreeable then to be in his company. If you went out to eat with him, he could hardly get a mouthful down and didn't speak a word. He had a Walkman with him and listened to Miles Davis constantly."

Carol Baker: "Chet did everything 100 percent. When he was home, he was the best family man one could imagine. But when he took drugs, then he was only the addict, then only the drugs mattered. Then he was sick, and nothing was to be done. But when he visited us in later years, he took nothing. He had so much respect in front of me and the children that he only took methadone pills for days. I gave him a lot of credit for that. Because it's very hard for an addict to escape the clutches of drugs. He found the willpower, in order not to disturb the order here."

Peter Huijts: "His moods were very variable. Everything came in extremes. You'd be sitting with him in a restaurant, and suddenly he would think of something that annoyed him. Something that had just happened, or something from the past. Insults and rage. Often, it was about money. Or because he had to wait for a glass of mineral water too long. That could disturb his equilibrium completely. He could express his fury more easily than his friendliness. His body and his spirit were not in unison. He could no longer process things rationally.

"Chet was never nervous before an appearance. He didn't have the least stage fright. But he could be ill-tempered on stage. When the music didn't go the way he wanted. But that also had a good side. He always tried to make the best of his time on stage. He never took it easy up there.

"During the concerts, he was often an especially agreeable person for the public. He took the trouble to introduce the musicians, announce the pieces, and generate the right mood. In that sense, he was an entertainer of the old school. Also to his fans, he could be very nice. I was always astonished at the way he had an open ear for everyone. Sometimes, people came with whole stacks of records that they wanted autographed. Chet autographed them all. He had a friendly word for everyone. He enjoyed the attention."

Harry Emmery: "Backstage was always full of people. People who asked him every imaginable thing about his past, people with cameras, people who wanted to do a record with him . . . Chet put up with all of it. He was very polite. He would sit down directly whenever somebody wanted to take a photo of him with his trumpet. Onstage, he was also very sociable. And singing—one of the reasons he did it was because he knew the public liked it. In order to communicate.

"I never heard Chet say anything negative about his colleagues. He never criticized his sidemen. Not as long as they were with him, anyway. If something went amiss, he often let it be known musically instead of verbally. Once Michel [Graillier] kept making a mistake in the form of a piece. He kept mixing up the first and the second half of the chord sequence. Chet didn't say anything and kept blowing, while making clear with his notes what the right chords were. Over and over. But Michel didn't respond. Finally Chet just started at the top with the theme—so that Michel had no choice but to hear it."

Wim Wigt: "In comparison with other American stars, I thought Chet was quite a regular guy. For many Americans, there is only Me, and other people are just accessories. 'We'll use him on drums, We'll use him on bass', etc. Chet was quite amiable. I found his behavior fairly normal. He was more adult than Stan Getz, for example. That whining by Getz, he was way above that. He made that impression, anyway. He reacted quite calmly when I told him that he couldn't complete the tour with Getz. It would have been very different the other way around.

"Of course, there's no doubt he had the usual desire for prestige. He wanted to determine the direction of the music. If there was another musician who wanted to dominate, that bothered him. I saw that with Philip Catherine. Chet cut off his partnership with him on the pretext that he didn't want to play with guitar any more. But, you know, Philip was something like the second star in the band. Since he was earning a lot, Chet was also getting less than usual—but I think the real reason was that Philip was having too much success. 'I don't need Philip Catherine,' he told me, a little annoyed. He was egocentric, but less than I experienced with other musicians. If he did not keep engagements, he was genuinely sorry. He was more human than most other musicians in those circumstances."

the recordings of chet baker: a select discography

$\mathcal{C}$het took part in very many recording sessions—too many, in fact. In revising the book for this edition I once more made a count—and came to more than 200. A complete description would be of interest only to the collector who wants to have them all. For that, I refer to "The Discography of Chesney Henry Baker" by Thorbjørn Sjøgren (Jazz Media, Copenhagen). This reasonably accurate discography covers nearly all the recordings issued before August 1993.

In the next chapter I take note of all Chet's records; in this chapter I cover the highlights—releases, that is, that are of artistic or historic importance, and on which Baker plays on most of the tracks. The availability of the issue also played a role in their selection. Discographical details are given; all releases are CD unless otherwise noted.

Live at the Trade Winds

Fresh Sound 1001

Chet Baker (tp); Sonny Criss (as); Wardell Gray, Dave Pell (ts); Jerry Mandell (p); Harry Babasin (cello); Bob Whitlock (b); Lawrence Marable (dr); 3/24/52.

Chet plays on "Out of Nowhere," his earliest recording. The rest of the tracks with different personnel. Only of historical interest.

Bird and Chet Live at the Trade Winds

Jazz Showcase 5007 (LP) / Fresh Sound CD 17

Chet Baker (tp); Charlie Parker, Sonny Criss (as); Al Haig (p); Russ Freeman (p, only on "Indiana"); Harry Babasin (b); Lawrence Marable (dr); 6/9/52:

THE SQUIRREL / THEY DIDN'T BELIEVE ME / INDIANA / LIZA

The Original Gerry Mulligan Quartet
with Chet Baker

Mosaic MR5-102 (LP) / MD3-102 (CD)

Chet Baker (tp); Gerry Mulligan (bs) with, among others, Bob Whitlock or Carson Smith (b) and Chico Hamilton or Larry Bunker (dr); 6/10/52–6/10/53

All the recordings that Mulligan's quartet and tentette made in this period for the Pacific label, collected in a box with several LPs/CDs. Chet is absent from the 6/10/52 session.

Gerry Mulligan
The Complete Pacific Jazz Recordings of the Gerry
Mulligan Quartet with Chet Baker

Pacific Jazz CDP 7243

A box containing four CDs. All the quartet recordings as found on the previously mentioned Mosaic box, but also including a guest appearance by Annie Ross (voc) and a reunion of Chet and Mulligan, both in December 1957.

On the recordings prior to his collaboration with Gerry Mulligan, the playing of our protagonist is not very compelling. So it is not quite clear why Charlie Parker was so taken with him. Chet has appealing ideas, but his technique lags behind.

The first notable recordings date from August 16, 1952. On that day, Chet and Mulligan recorded "Lullaby of the Leaves" and "Bernie's Tune." The tender trumpet sound, the apparently hesitant phrasing, the extremely melodic lines—all these are distinctively here already. Record buyers liked what they heard, and this single was the breakthrough for both horn players. "My Funny Valentine" became an even bigger success. It is interesting to note that on his earliest recordings Chet still uses an old-fashioned vibrato. One hears the influence of Harry James—the first jazz trumpeter that Chet knew—and of the army bands.

More beautiful still than the hit version of September 1952 is the live recording from May 1953, which can be found in the Mosaic box. The trumpeter improvises here with burning intensity. After his first chorus, one can tell by the hesitant way Mulligan follows that it is as if he were thinking, Well, what can I add to that? But all the trumpeter does is play the melody, with a few small variations.

In general, however, these recordings don't have the depth of their later playing. Baker had to grow as a soloist, and Mulligan still sounds like an apprentice. One can practically hear him thinking: After A minor comes D7 with a minor ninth, and so forth. The boxes on Mosaic and Pacific Jazz are in general ideally edited: all recordings for Pacific are collected here, including many previously unreleased tracks. The booklet includes photos and lots of background information.

The Complete Pacific Jazz Studio
Chet Baker/Russ Freeman

Mosaic MR4-122 (LP) / MD3-122 (CD)

Chet Baker (tp, voc); Russ Freeman (p); Bob Whitlock, Carson Smith, Joe Mondragon, Jimmy Bond or Leroy Vinnegar (b), Bobby White, Larry Bunker, Shelly Manne, Bob Neel, Lawrence Marable or Peter Littman (dr); 7/24/53–11/6/56.

All studio recordings of Freeman and Baker for the Pacific label in a box containing several LPs/CDs.

Chet Baker Ensemble and Sextet

Fresh Sound FSR-CD 175

Baker (tp) with (among others) Jack Montrose (ts), Herb Geller (as, ts),

Bud Shank (bs), Bob Brookmeyer (valve tb), Russ Freeman (p), Shelly Manne (d), December 1953, and September, 1954 (only the last song by a Chet Baker Quintet, 1956):
BOCKHANAL (2x) / ERGO / MOONLIGHT BECOMES YOU / HEADLINE / A DANDY LINE / LITTLE OLD LADY / GOODBYE (2x) / PRO DEFUNCTUS / THE HALF DOZENS / I'M GLAD THERE'S YOU / STELLA BY STARLIGHT / TOMMY HAWK / LITTLE MAN YOU'VE HAD A BUSY DAY / DOT'S GROOVY / MUSIC TO DANCE TO

Chet Baker
The Best of Chet Baker Sings

Pacific Jazz / Capitol Records; CDP 7 92932 2

Chet Baker (tp, voc), Russ Freeman (p), Joe Mondragon, Carson Smith or Jimmy Bond (b), Shelly Manne, Bob Neel, Peter Littman, or Lawrence Marable (dr); 10/27/53–7/30/1956.

Contains all recordings of *Chet Baker Sings* (2/15/1954 and 7/23, 30/1956—see below), but a different take of "The Thrill is Gone"; also:
DAYBREAK / JUST FRIENDS / I REMEMBER YOU / LET'S GET LOST / LONG AGO AND FAR AWAY / YOU DON'T KNOW WHAT LOVE IS

The collaboration with Russ Freeman is also documented on very many releases. Many tracks, moreover, turn up on miscellaneous compilations. Whoever is interested only in the highlights from the first records as singer will find an excellent selection in the above-mentioned CD. It is to be preferred to *Chet Baker Sings*, since the latter contains less music, and is diminished by a good deal of echo and a guitar that was added to the mix a year later.

Chet sang in these years with a boyish, innocent voice,

and the accompaniment is restrained. But the innocence is apparent only. The song "Look for the Silver Lining" has a sad atmosphere underneath the happy, 'Always look at the bright side of life'-lyrics. And when Chet recites the words of "I Fall in Love Too Easily," one can practically sense his imminent fate. Some go into raptures over these recordings, others abhor his singing, but this music leaves no one cold. The trumpet solos in the studio are frequently miniature compositions in themselves: intense and yet precisely calibrated solos, in which not a note is otiose.

Almost all extant recordings of the Baker/Freeman quartet —including, of course, the music on this CD—are contained in both of the Mosaic boxes: *The Complete Pacific Jazz Live* and *The Complete Pacific Jazz Studio.* Comparison proves that the musicians played with more concentration in the studio. On the live recordings, the trumpeter sounds a little flat in the fast tempos, and Freeman plays uninspired here and there. The pianist in the booklet of the Mosaic box of the studio recordings: "Some of the things that I wrote I still like. 'Bea's Flat,' I think is good . . . 'The Wind' is a good song . . . and I like 'Summer Sketch.' I'm more pleased, I think with the things that I wrote than with the way I was playing in those days. I liked my playing better later on."

Chet Baker
Chet Baker Sings

Pacific Jazz CJ-32-5005

Chet Baker (tp, voc), Russ Freeman (p), Carson Smith or Jimmy Bond (b), Bob Neel, Peter Littman or Lawrence Marable (dr); 2/15/54, 7/23,

30/56:

BUT NOT FOR ME / TIME AFTER TIME / I GET ALONG WITHOUT YOU
VERY WELL / THERE WILL NEVER BE ANOTHER YOU / LOOK FOR THE
SILVER LINING / MY FUNNY VALENTINE / I FALL IN LOVE TOO EASILY /
THE THRILL IS GONE / THAT OLD FEELING / IT'S ALWAYS YOU / I'VE
NEVER BEEN IN LOVE BEFORE / MY BUDDY / MY IDEAL / LIKE SOME-
ONE IN LOVE

The Complete Pacific Jazz Live
Chet Baker/Russ Freeman

MOSAIC MR4-113 (LP) / MD3-113 (CD)

Chet Baker (tp), Russ Freeman (p), Carson Smith (b), Bob Neel (dr);
5/9/54–summer or fall 1954: All live recordings of this quartet for
Pacific in a box with several LPs/CDs.

Chet Baker Sings and Plays

Pacific Jazz CP 32-5352

Chet Baker (tp), Bud Shank (fl), Russ Freeman (p), Red Mitchell (b),
Bob Neel (dr), strings; 2/28/1955: THIS IS ALWAYS / SOMEONE TO
WATCH OVER ME / GREY DECEMBER / I WISH I KNEW

Personnel as 5/9/1954; 3/7/1955: DAYBREAK / JUST FRIENDS / I
REMEMBER YOU / LET'S GET LOST / LONG AGO AND FAR AWAY / YOU
DON'T KNOW WHAT LOVE IS

Chet Baker
Chet in Paris Vol. 1

EmArcy 837 474-2

Chet Baker (tp), Dick Twardzik (p), Jimmy Bond (b), Peter Littman (dr);
10/11, 14/1955: RONDETTE / MID-FORTE / SAD WALK / RESEARCH /
JUST DUO / PIECE CAPRICE / POMP / THE GIRL FROM GREENLAND /
BRASH

Chet Baker (tp), Benny Vasseur (tb), Jean Aldegon (as), René Urtreger (p), Jimmy Bond (b), Nils-Bert Dahlander (dr); 10/25/1955: CHET / DINAH / V LINE / IN MEMORY OF DICK

Chet in Paris Vol. 2

EmArcy 837 475-2

Chet Baker (tp), Gérard Gustin (p), Jimmy Bond (b), Nils-Bert Dahlander (dr); 10/24/1955: SUMMERTIME / YOU GO TO MY HEAD / TENDERLY / LOVER MAN / THERE'S A SMALL HOTEL / AUTUMN IN NEW YORK / THESE FOOLISH THINGS / I'LL REMEMBER APRIL

Chet Baker (tp, voc), Raymond Fol (p), Benoît Quersin (b), Jean-Louis Viale (dr), 11/28/1955: ALONE TOGETHER / EXITUS / ONCE IN A WHILE / ALL THE THINGS YOU ARE / EVERYTHING HAPPENS TO ME

Chet in Paris Vol. 3

EmArcy 837 476-2

Chet Baker (tp), Bobby Jaspar (ts), René Urtreger (p), Benoît Quersin (b), Jean-Louis Viale (dr), 12/16/1955: CHEKEETAH / HOW ABOUT YOU / EXITUS / DEAR OLD STOCKHOLM

Chet Baker (tp), Jean-Louis Chautemps (ts), Francy Boland (p), Eddie de Haas (b), Charles Saudrais (dr); 2/10/1956: SPEAK LOW / ANTICI-PATED BLUES / CHERYL / TASTY PUDDING

Personnel as 2/10/1956, except Pierre Lemarchand (dr) instead of Charles Saudrais, and add Benny Vasseur (tb), Teddy Ameline (as), Armand Migiani (ts), William Boucaya (bs); 3/15/1956: MYTHE / NOT TOO SLOW / V LINE / IN A LITTLE PROVINCIAL TOWN

Chet in Paris Vol. 4

EmArcy 837 477-2

Personnel as 10/25/1955 (same session):

CHET / DINAH / IN MEMORY OF DICK

Personnel as 11/18/1955 (same session):
ALONE TOGETHER (2x) / EXITUS / ALL THE THINGS YOU ARE

Personnel as 12/16/1955 (same session):
CHEKEETAH / HOW ABOUT YOU / EXITUS (2x)

Personnel as 2/10/1956 (same session)
ANTICIPATED BLUES / TASTY PUDDING (4x)

The Barclay label has collectively released all their recordings with Chet. The recording quality is good, but the accompanying text leaves something to be desired; e.g. "Everything Happens to Me" (Vol. 2), is certainly not Chet's first recording as singer, as the notes would have it.

Chet's playing in this first European period is inconsistent. The causes are well known: He has difficulties with his teeth, with his French girlfriend, with drugs, and also with his sidemen—in those years European jazz musicians weren't very good.

The most interesting sessions are those with Dick Twardzik (Vol. 1). The quartet plays compositions by Bob Zieff, a friend of Twardzik, who like him came from Boston. The pieces have a structure that fundamentally deviates from that of the jazz standards of the time, and were influenced by classical compositions. The leader is in best form on the medium-fast "Sad Walk." This piece would remain in his repertoire until his death. On the odd themes and the uncommon chord changes Twardzik acquits himself better than the trumpeter.

Chet Baker
Cools Out

Pacific Jazz/Boplicity BOP 13

Chet Baker (tp), Phil Urso (ts), Bobby Timmons (p), Jimmy Bond (b), Peter Littman (dr), 7/31/1956:

LUCIUS LOU / PAWNEE JUNCTION / EXTRA MILD / HALEMA / JUMPIN' OFF A CLIFF

Chet Baker (tp), Art Pepper (as), Richie Kamuca (ts), Pete Jolly (p), Leroy Vinnegar (b), Stan Levey (dr), 7/26/1956:
THE ROUTE

Note: Halema is incorrectly identified on the cover as 'Helena.'

Chet Baker
Chet Baker & Crew

Pacific Jazz 781205

Baker (tp, voc), Phil Urso (ts), Bobby Timmons (p), Jimmy Bond (b), Peter Littman (d), (on a few tracks) Bill Loughbrough (perc); July, 1956:

TO MICKEY'S MEMORY (2x) / SLIGHTLY ABOVE MODERATE / HALEMA / REVELATION / SOMETHING FOR LIZA / LUCIUS LOU / WORRYIN' THE LIFE OUT OF ME / MEDIUM ROCK / JUMPIN' OFF A CLEF / CHIPPYIN' / PAWNEE JUNCTION / MUSIC TO DANCE BY / LINE FOR LYONS

Chet Baker/Art Pepper
Playboys

Pacific Jazz CDP 7944742

Chet Baker (tp), Art Pepper (as), Phil Urso (ts), Carl Perkins (p), Curtis Counce (b), Lawrence Marable (dr); 10/31/1956:

FOR MINORS ONLY / MINOR YOURS / RESONANT EMOTIONS / TYNAN TIME / PICTURE OF HEATH / FOR MILES AND MILES / CTA

Chet Baker/Russ Freeman Quartet

Pacific Jazz CP 32-5362

Chet Baker (tp), Russ Freeman (p), Leroy Vinnegar (b), Shelly Manne (dr); 11/6/1956:

LOVE NEST / FAN TAN / SUMMER SKETCH / AN AFTERNOON AT HOME / SAY WHEN / LUSH LIFE / AMBLIN' / HUGO HURWHEY

Freeman got the offer to record as leader. He hired the rhythm section of Shelly Manne's combo—which he belonged to at the time—and his earlier collaborator Chet Baker. A terrific lineup, which resulted in bop without clichés. Despite lip problems, Baker blows solos bursting with ideas, and the rhythm section follows him in hot pursuit. Freeman had grown as an arranger, composer, and pianist. (This record can also be found in the Mosaic box with Baker and Freeman's studio recordings.)

Gerry Mulligan Quartet

Manhattan CDP 7 46857 2

Chet Baker (tp), Gerry Mulligan (bs), Henry Grimes (b), Dave Bailey (dr); 11/3 and 12/17/1957:

REUNION / WHEN YOUR LOVER HAS GONE / STARDUST / MY HEART BELONGS TO DADDY / JERSEY BOUNCE / THE SURREY WITH THE FRINGE ON TOP / TRAV'LIN LIGHT (2x) / ORNITHOLOGY / PEOPLE WILL SAY WE'RE IN LOVE / THE SONG IS YOU / GEE BABY, AIN'T I GOOD TO YOU (2x) / I GOT RHYTHM / ALL THE THINGS YOU ARE

Note: This CD contains substantially more music than the original LP release. These sessions are also included in the box *The Complete Pacific Jazz Recordings of The Gerry Mulligan Quartet with Chet Baker.*

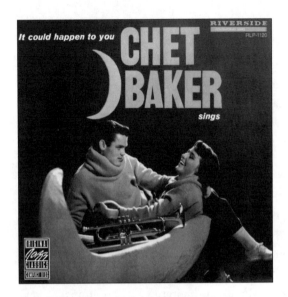

Chet Baker Sings It Could Happen to You

Original Jazz Classics OJCCD 303-2

Chet Baker (voc, tp), Kenny Drew (p), Sam Jones or George Morrow
(b), Philly Joe Jones or Dannie Richmond (dr); August 1958:
DO IT THE HARD WAY / I'M OLD FASHIONED / YOU'RE DRIVING ME
CRAZY / IT COULD HAPPEN TO YOU / MY HEART STOOD STILL / THE
MORE I SEE YOU / EVERYTHING HAPPENS TO ME / DANCING ON THE
CEILING / HOW LONG HAS THIS BEEN GOING ON? / OLD DEVIL MOON /
WHILE MY LADY SLEEPS / YOU MAKE ME FEEL SO YOUNG
Note: The last two titles on CD only

Chet Baker
In New York

Original Jazz Classics OJCCD 207-2

Chet Baker (tp), Johnny Griffin (ts), Al Haig (p), Paul Chambers (b),
Philly Joe Jones (dr); September 1958:
FAIR WEATHER / POLKA DOTS AND MOONBEAMS / HOTEL 49 / SOLAR /
BLUE THOUGHTS / WHEN LIGHTS ARE LOW

In 1958, Chet began recording with Riverside. This label was not altogether clear on how to best position Chet in the market and allowed him to record four very different records. The trumpeter had many problems in these years, which explains his uninspired playing. There are two exceptions: *It Could Happen to You* and *In New York*. The former, although falling short of his debut record as a singer, still has many beautiful moments, particularly during light-footed songs like "Dancing on the Ceiling" and "You Make Me Feel So Young" (the latter on CD only). *New York* is a genuine hard-bop outing, on which the trumpeter holds his own alongside aggressive East Coast blowers like Johnny Griffin.

Chet Baker
In Milan

OJCCD 370-2

Chet Baker (tp), Glauco Masetti (as), Gianni Basso (ts), Renato Sellani (p), Franco Cerri (b), Gene Victory (dr); 9/25, 26/59 and 10/6/59: LOOK FOR THE SILVER LINING / LADY BIRD / MY OLD FLAME / LINE FOR LYONS / TUNE UP / CHERYL / INDIAN SUMMER / PENT UP HOUSE

Chet Baker
Chet Is Back

RCA CL 31649 (LP)

Chet Baker (tp), Bobby Jaspar (ts), René Thomas (g), Amadeo Tommasi (p), Benoît Quersin (b), Daniel Humair (dr), 2/5/1962: WELL YOU NEEDN'T / THESE FOOLISH THINGS / BARBADOS / STAR EYES / OVER THE RAINBOW / PENT UP HOUSE / BALLATE IN FORMA DI BLUES / BLUES IN THE CLOSET

Note: also under the name *The Italian Sessions* (RCA Bluebird ND 82001

This is the best record—and overall one of the few satis-factory ones from beginning to end—between *Quartet* (11/6/1956) and *She Was Too Good to Me* (July/October/November 1974). In the course of the '60s Baker lost his popularity, his confidence, his trumpet (he switched to flugelhorn), and his teeth. But this recording, made soon after his release from prison, still sounds hopeful. His bittersweet solo on "Over the Rainbow" and his powerful playing on the bop classics made this record a popular as well as a critical success. His accompanists are among the best to be found in Europe at the time.

Chet Baker
Plays and Sings

Jazz Junction JJ 205

Chet Baker (flh), Phil Urso (ts), Hal Galper (p), Jymie Merritt (b), Charlie Rice (dr), 6/1/1964:

SOULTRANE / WALKIN' / TADD'S DELIGHT / WHATEVER POSSESSED
ME / RETSIM B. / GNID / ANN, WONDERFUL ONE / MATING CALL /
MARGERINE / FLIGHT TO JORDAN

Chet Baker
Baby Breeze

Verve 538 328-2

Chet Baker (voc), Bobby Scott (p), Kenny Burrell (g), 1/20/1965:
YOU'RE MINE, YOU / EVERYTHING DEPENDS ON YOU / BORN TO BE
BLUE / SWEET SUE / TASTE OF HONEY

Chet Baker (flh), Phil Urso (ts), Frank Strozier (as), Hal Galper (p),
Michael Fleming (b), Charlie Rice (dr); 2/14/1965:
PAMELA'S PASSION / BABY BREEZE / THIS IS THE THING / COMIN'
DOWN / ONE WITH ONE

Personnel as 2/14/65; Bob James replaces Hal Galper; without Urso
and Strozier; 2/20/65:
THE TOUCH OF YOUR LIPS / THINK BEAUTIFUL / I WISH YOU LOVE

Chet Baker
Baker's Holiday

EmArcy 838204 / Trip TLP 5569

Chet Baker (voc, flh), with a ten-piece orchestra, including Hank Jones
(p), Richard Davis (b), and Connie Kay (dr), May or June 1965:
TRAV'LIN' LIGHT / EASY LIVING / THAT OLD DEVIL CALLED LOVE /
YOU'RE MY THRILL / CRAZY SHE CALLS ME / WHEN YOUR LOVER HAS
GONE / MEAN TO ME / THESE FOOLISH THINGS / THERE IS NO
GREATER LOVE / DON'T EXPLAIN

Another point of light in these dark times. Jimmy
Mundy's arrangements are sometimes a bit slick, but
Chet succeeds in making a worthy tribute to Billie

Holiday from them. Billie Holiday's repertoire—strong melodies like "Mean to Me" and "Don't Explain"—seems to suit him.

Chet Baker
Lonely Star
Prestige PRCD 24172-2

Chet Baker (flh), George Coleman (ts), Kirk Lightsey (p), Herman Wright (b); Roy Brooks (dr); 8/23, 25, 29/65:
MADISON AVENUE / LONELY STAR / WEE, TOO / TAN GAUGIN / GRADE 'A' GRAVY / SERENITY / FINE AND DANDY / HAVE YOU MET MISS JONES? / REARIN' BACK / SO EASY

Stairway to the Stars
Prestige PRCD 24173-2

personnel and dates as above
CHEROKEE / BEVAN BEEPS / COMIN' ON / STAIRWAY TO THE STARS / NO FAIR LADY / WHEN YOU'RE GONE / CHOOSE NOW / CHABOOTIE / CARPSIE'S GROOVE / I WAITED FOR YOU / THE 490

On a Misty Night
Prestige PSCD 24174-2

personnel and dates as above
CUT PLUG / BOUDOIR / ETUDE IN THREE / SLEEPING SUSAN / GO-GO / LAMENT FOR THE LIVING / POT LUCK / BUD'S BLUES / ROMAS / ON A MISTY NIGHT / HURRY

Note: The three above-mentioned CDs contain all the music from the earlier LPs *Groovin'*, *Comin' on*, *Smokin'*, *Cool Burnin'* and *Boppin'*.

Chet Baker
Live at Pueblo, Colorado

CC Baker CCB 12225

Baker (flh, voc), Phil Urso (ts), Dave McKay (p), Chuck Domanico (b), Harry Keevis Jr. (d); summer 1966:

AIREGIN / ROUND MIDNIGHT / ON GREEN DOLPHIN STREET / LUCIUS LOU / MR. B / FORGETFUL / MILESTONES / LUCIUS LU

A rare live recording with real jazz in these difficult times, showing that Baker was still able to play hard-driving and deeply felt music while trying to make a living with bands like the Mariachi Brass. Carol Baker issued the recordings in the '90s on her own label. The recording quality is bearable.

Chet Baker
She Was Too Good To Me

EPIC EPC 450954 2

Chet Baker (voc, tp) Paul Desmond (as), Hubert Laws (fl), Bob James (e-p), Ron Carter (b), Jack DeJohnette or Steve Gadd (dr), strings on some tracks; 7/17, 10/31, 11/1/74:

AUTUMN LEAVES / TANGERINE / FUNK IN DEEP FREEZE / WITH A SONG IN MY HEART / IT'S YOU OR NO ONE / SHE WAS TOO GOOD TO ME / WHAT'LL I DO / MY FUTURE JUST PASSED

Comment: the last track on CD only

Gerry Mulligan /Chet Baker
Carnegie Hall Concert

Epic ZK 64769

Chet Baker (voc, tp) Gerry Mulligan (bs), Ed Byrne (tb), Rob James (p, e-p), David Samuels (vib), John Scofield (g), Ron Carter (b), Harvey Mason (dr), 11/24/74:

LINE FOR LYONS / SONG FOR AN UNFINISHED WOMAN / MY FUNNY
VALENTINE / SONG FOR STRAYHORN / IT'S SANDY AT THE BEACH /
BERNIE'S ACTION / K4 PACIFIC / THERE WILL NEVER BE ANOTHER
YOU / MARGERINE

Jim Hall
Concierto
Epic ZK65132
Chet Baker (tp), Paul Desmond (as), Jim Hall (g), Roland Hanna (p),
Ron Carter (b), Steve Gadd (dr); April 1975:
YOU'D BE SO NICE TO COME HOME TO / TWO'S BLUES / THE ANSWER
IS YES / CONCIERTO DE ARANJUEZ / ROCK SKIPPIN ' / UNFINISHED
BUSINESS / YOU'D BE SO NICE TO COME HOME TO

Creed Taylor, producer of the distinguished label CTI,
tried to do some business with the born-again trumpeter
and got him into the studio several times in the '70s. The
first record on CTI is the best of the series. A lot of time
and money was expended on the production, and it
shows. The energetic playing of drummer Steve Gadd
thunders behind the fragile trumpet sounds, and one
would gladly forego the strings, but otherwise there is little to fault. A beautiful, popular record.

Less successful is the reunion with Mulligan, on which
the trumpeter gets much too little solo space, while the
session with Jim Hall is partly spoiled by an unnecessar-
ily long treatment of the "Concierto de Aranjuez."

Chet Baker
Once Upon a Summertime
OJCCD OJC-405
Chet Baker (tp), Gregory Herbert (ts), Harold Danko (p), Ron Carter

(b), Mel Lewis (dr); 2/20/77:
TIDAL BREEZE / SHIFTING DOWN / ESP / THE SONG IS YOU / ONCE
UPON A SUMMERTIME

Never would Chet's playing resemble the playing of
Miles Davis as much as on this record, above all on the
blues "Shifting Down" where he plays a solo with mute.
The solos by Gregory Herbert are permeated by Coltrane
licks, reinforcing further still the Miles atmosphere.
(Herbert died the following year in Amsterdam at the age
of 30.) Unfortunately, the title piece runs on too long,
and Ron Carter's bass is recorded too loudly.

Chet Baker
You Can't Go Home Again

A&M CD 0805 / 396997 2

Chet Baker (tp), Michael Brecker (ts), Paul Desmond (as), Hubert Laws
(fl, bf, picc), John Scofield (g), Richie Beirach, Don Sebesky or Kenny
Barron (keyb), Ron Carter (b), Alphonso Jackson (e-b), Tony Williams
(dr), Ralph McDonald (perc), strings; 2/16, 21, 22/1977, 5/13/77:
LOVE FOR SALE / UN POCO LOCO / YOU CAN'T GO HOME AGAIN / EL
MORRO

Chet Baker
The Best Thing for You

A&M CD 0832

personnel and dates as above; Gary Bertoncini (g) on "If You Could
See Me Now":
THE BEST THING FOR YOU / I'M GETTING SENTIMENTAL OVER YOU /
OH YOU CRAZY MOON / HOW DEEP IS THE OCEAN / IF YOU COULD
SEE ME NOW / EL MORRO

On *You Can't Go Home Again* the trumpeter is surrounded by young jazz-rock stars. With Michael Brecker he can be heard on three long, tightly arranged titles, while Paul Desmond accompanies him on the title piece, a ballad. Chet has to adapt himself a little, but is proud of the result: he considered this one of his best records, and it is notable how he was able to assert himself alongside his young, energetic sidemen.

Don Sebesky's arrangement of "Love for Sale" he would play up to his death again and again, and "You Can't Go Home Again" also remained in his repertoire. Some successful, but initially unreleased titles from these sessions appeared after Baker's death on the CD *The Best Thing For You*.

Chet Baker
Broken Wing

Cornelia/ADDA 581020

Chet Baker (tp, voc), Phil Markowitz (p), Jean-François Jenny-Clark (b), Jeff Brillinger (dr); 12/28/1978:
BROKEN WING / BEAUTIFUL BLACK EYES / OH YOU CRAZY MOON / HOW DEEP IS THE OCEAN / BLUE GILLES

Note: Re-released on CD as *In Paris Vol. 2* (West Wind 2059). The cover of this reissue gives an incorrect recording date and wrongly suggests that it is a live recording.

Toward the end of 1978, Chet undertook a European tour with the American pianist Phil Markowitz. This quartet did a whole series of records, among which *Broken Wing* stands out. Here, an impetuous fusion

245

drummer and the booming bass of Ron Carter are replaced by cautious sounds of kindred souls, who do everything for the musical well-being of their leader. Markowitz grounds every fragile trumpet note with a resonant chord, and the bass player and the drummer go on tiptoe.

It is noteworthy that less and less of his increasingly chaotic life is reflected in Chet's music. This is peaceful music, on which almost complete calm prevails—the unreal silence after a summer thunderstorm, the silence of a February morning, on which all sounds are muffled in the snow. Chet has turned to junk again, he is 'tough' (Rocky Knauer), 'egocentric' (Wim Wigt); he neglects his family and makes life for Diane difficult—but in his music there is no aggression. "He could express his anger more easily than his friendliness," according to Peter Huijts, but as soon as Chet put the trumpet to his lips, exactly the opposite was the case.

Chet Baker
The Touch of Your Lips
Steeplechase SCCD 31122
Chet Baker (voc, tp) Doug Raney (g), Niels-Henning Ørsted-Pedersen (b); 6/21/1979:
I WAITED FOR YOU / BUT NOT FOR ME / AUTUMN IN NEW YORK / BLUE ROOM / THE TOUCH OF YOUR LIPS / STAR EYES

Chet Baker
Round Midnight
Challenge Records CHR 70052
Chet Baker (voc, tp), Jean Paul Florens (g), Henry Florens (p), Jim

Richardson (b), Tony Mann (dr); 9/4-5/1979:
BLUES FOR INGE / WHAT'S NEW / DARN THAT DREAM / MY FUNNY
VALENTINE / SECRET LOVE / PHIL'S BOSSA / ROUND MIDNIGHT

Personnel as 9/4–5/1979; add Rachel Gould (voc); 9/5/79:
ALL BLUES / STRAIGHT, NO CHASER / ROUND MIDNIGHT

Most pieces appeared on the CD Celluloid CEL 6780
under the title Chet Baker 79.

Chet Baker
No Problem

Steeplechase SCCD 31131

Chet Baker (tp), Duke Jordan (p), Niels-Henning Ørsted Pedersen (b),
Norman Fearrington (dr); 10/2/1979:
NO PROBLEM / SULTRY EYE / GLAD I MET PAT / KISS OF SPAIN / THE
FUZZ / MY QUEEN IS HOME TO STAY / JEALOUS BLUES

Chet Baker
Daybreak

Steeplechase SCCD 31442

Personnel as 6/21/1979; 10/4/1979:
FOR MINORS ONLY / DAYBREAK / YOU CAN'T GO HOME AGAIN /
BROKEN WING / DOWN

This Is Always

Steeplechase SCCD 31168

same session as 10/4/1979:
HOW DEEP IS THE OCEAN / HOUSE OF JADE / LOVE FOR SALE / THIS
IS ALWAYS / LUCIUS LU

Note: The last number is erroneously identified on the
cover as "Way to Go Out."

Someday My Prince Will Come

Steeplechase SCCD 31180

same Session as 10/4/1979: GNID / LOVE VIBRATIONS / SAD WALK /
SOMEDAY MY PRINCE WILL COME / I'M OLD FASHIONED / IN YOUR
OWN SWEET WAY

Chet's inconsistency was notorious. I have attended
dozens of concerts by Chet, many of them pitifully poor.
But on October 4, 1979 he made in one evening in
Copenhagen enough good music to fill three (outstanding) LPs. And when the music was later brought out on
CD, some excellent bonus tracks were added. The trumpet sound is quiet, but clear. Chet's chops for once
appear to have not left him in the lurch. Raney's accompaniment is a little dull at times, but that does not seem
to disturb the leader. *The Touch of Your Lips*—in the
same lineup—is also commendable, as is *No Problem,*
which shows how well the compositions of Duke Jordan
suited Chet.

Chet Baker
Why Shouldn't You Cry

Enja ENJ 9337 2

Baker (tp, voc) and Wolfgang Lackerschmid (vibes, perc) in diverse
groups, with, among others, Buster Williams (b), Tony Williams (d) and
Larry Coryell (g); 1979–1987:

WHY SHOULDN'T YOU CRY / YOU DON'T KNOW WHAT LOVE IS / RUE
GREGOIRE DU TOUR / BALZWALTZ / FIVE YEARS AGO / WALTZ FOR
BERLIN / DESSERT / TOKU DO / CHET'S BALLAD

The German vibes player Wolfgang Lackerschmid made a couple of recordings with Chet. Luckily, only the best tracks are put on this compilation. It contains some fragile, charming melodies. In a couple of tracks, the two play a kind of mellow free jazz, which seemed to have been no big deal at all for Chet; improvising by ear had been his specialty all along.

Chet Baker Quartet
Burnin' at Backstreet

Fresh Sound FSR-CD 128

Baker (tp), Drew Salperto (p), Mike Formanek (b), Art Frank (d);
February 19, 1980(?):
TUNE UP / MILESTONES / BLUE 'N BOOGIE / STELLA BY STARLIGHT /
FOUR / JUST FRIENDS

The date cited seems improbable, as Chet was in Europe

immediately before and after that day. In any case, he sounds as if he had to prove to someone in the room that he could play loud, fast and high if he wanted to, without watering down his distinctive style. The sound is not perfect, and the band sounds a bit ragged, but the fine drummer Art Frank—who had been working with Chet in the US since the '60s—knows how to push him without pushing him too hard.

Chet Baker
Leaving

Intercord INT 160 154 (LP)

Chet Baker (tp), Nicola Stilo (fl), Dennis Luxion (p), Ricardo Del Fra (b); April 1980:

GERSHWIN GOES TO RIO / LEAVING / YOU'VE FLIPPED OUT / TEMPUS FUGIT / BLUES FOR C.R. / PRAYER FOR THE NEWBORN / WHEN I FALL IN LOVE

Intercord shows with this production that they could do also a record that is successful from beginning to end with the same personnel as on the chaotic Circle albums. The solos of the sidemen are kept short, and the tape recorder waited until Chet got his lips in working order. The band doesn't simply revisit the old repertoire but interprets four compositions of the young pianist Dennis Luxion full of concentration. A restrained, solemn mood prevails.

Ron Carter
Patrao

Milestone M 9099 (LP)

Chet Baker (tp), Kenny Barron (p), Ron Carter (b), Jack DeJohnette (dr); 5/19, 20/80:

NEARLY / TAIL FEATHERS / YOURS TRULY

Personnel and dates as above, but Edison Machado replaces DeJohnette, and add Amaury Tristaos (g), Aloisio Aguiar (p), Nana Vasconcelos (perc):

AH, RIO / THIRD PLANE

Chet Baker

Carlyne CAR CD 15

Chet Baker (voc, tp), René Urtreger (p), Pierre Michelot (b), Aldo Romano (dr); 11/3/1981:

FOR MINORS ONLY / CHASIN' THE BIRD / BUT NOT FOR ME / DOWN / MY FUNNY VALENTINE / JUST FRIENDS

Chet Baker
But Not For Me

Stash ST-CD-584

Baker (tp, voc), James Newton (fl), Howard Johnson (tuba), Kenny Barron (p), Charlie Haden (b), Ben Riley (d); 4/1/82:

LAMENT / FOUR / LINE FOR LYONS / ELLEN DAVID / BUT NOT FOR ME / PRAYER FOR THE NEWBORN

Note: The song called "Lament" on this record is not the same tune as the J.J. Johnson ballad Chet also used to play in later years.

A rare thing in this period: an American studio recording. The level is not exceptional but the results are enjoyable enough. Haden is just as subtle a musician as Chet, and Johnson demonstrates how to play bebop choruses on the tuba. The tapes were laying in archives for a long time before they were finally committed to record in 1994.

Stan Getz/Chet Baker

Chet Baker (voc, tp), Stan Getz (ts), Jim McNeely (p), George Mraz (b),
Victor Lewis (dr); 2/18/83:
JUST FRIENDS (2x) / STELLA BY STARLIGHT / AIREGIN (2x) / MY
FUNNY VALENTINE (2x) / MILESTONES / DEAR OLD STOCKHOLM /
LINE FOR LYONS / SIPPIN' AT BELL'S (2x)

Note: Chet does not play on the rest of the tracks.

Three CDs, containing two concerts Baker and Getz did
in a single day. Chet is on half of the tracks, but he only
really plays together with Getz on two of them: "Line for
Lyons" (breathtakingly done without rhythm section) and
the wonderful "Dear Old Stockholm," where Chet seems
to lose track of the chord structure but plays majestical-
ly nevertheless.

Chet Baker
Mr. B.

Timeless CDSJP 192

Chet Baker (voc, tp), Kirk Lightsey (p), David Eubanks (b), Eddie
Gladden (dr), 3/14/1983:
RAY'S IDEA / EVERYTHING HAPPENS TO ME

Chet Baker (tp), Michel Graillier (p), Ricardo Del Fra (b); 5/25/83:
DOLPHIN DANCE / ELLEN AND DAVID / STROLLIN' / IN YOUR OWN
SWEET WAY / MISTER B. / BEATRICE

Note: "Mister B." is the same piece as "Retsim B."
(spelling reversed; cf. *Chet Baker Plays and Sings*, 1964).

In the enclosed text, some songs are presented as Chet
Baker originals. Actually none of the tunes were composed by him.

There is another *Mr. B.* reissue (also as Timeless SJP 192) that, besides the 3/14/1983 session contains two pieces from the interrupted session: "White Blues" (10/4/85) and "Father Xmas" with Philip Catherine (12/20/85). The liner notes misleadingly suggest that all the pieces derive from the same session.

On the March 14, 1983 session Chet plays with Dexter Gordon's rhythm section. Gordon was supposed to participate, but got lost in Amsterdam in an alcoholic fog. Both these pieces originally appeared on an LP that was supplemented by recordings of Lightsey's trio. One may hear the emphasis that the lyric of "Everything Happens to Me" gets. I had heard the piece often already, but only now did its significance become clear.

Chet sounds tired on the trio session—little wonder, since he had driven straight through from Italy to Holland without a break. Still, he plays the themes with an almost religious dedication, so that one thinks: no one will dare interpret this piece afterward.

Chet Baker
The Improviser

Cadence CJR 1019

Chet Baker (tp), Per Husby (p), Bjørn Kjellemyr (b), Espen Rud (dr); 8/15/1983:

GNID / NIGHT BIRD

Chet Baker (tp), Per Husby (p), Terje Venaas (b), Ole Jacob Hansen (dr); 8/30/1983:

MARGERINE / POLKA DOTS AND MOONBEAMS / BEATRICE

A completely different mood. Everything goes wrong. Chet plays on a borrowed trumpet, the rhythm section plays in the wrong key once—but that cannot stop Chet. He turns out here as aggressive bebopper, who doesn't shy from fast tempi and excursions into the high register. The methadone helps him apparently. At the end of one of these concerts, he says, "I think I could polish off one whole pizza alone." He is mistaken: according to the liner notes, it takes two.

Rassinfosse/Baker/Catherine

Igloo IGL 034

Chet Baker (tp), Philip Catherine, (g), Jean-Louis Rassinfosse (b); September 1983:

CRYSTAL BELLS / STROLLIN' / LAMENT / LEAVING / CHEROKEE / ESTATE

Chet Baker
Live in Sweden

Dragon DRCD 178

Chet Baker (tp, voc), Åke Johansson (p), Kjell Jansson (b), Göran Levin (dr); 9/29/1983:

LAMENT / MY IDEAL / BEATRICE / ELLEN AND DAVID / YOU CAN'T GO HOME AGAIN / RAY'S IDEA / MILESTONES / BUT NOT FOR ME

Chet Baker
Al Capolinea

Red Records NS 206 (LP)

Chet Baker (tp), Nicola Stilo (fl), Diane Vavra (ss), Michel Graillier (p), Ricardo Del Fra (b), Leo Mitchell (dr); October 1983:

ESTATE / FRANCAMENTE / DREAM DROP / LAMENT / PIOGGIA SUL DESERTO / FINESTRA SUL MARE

Chet Baker/Warne Marsh
Blues for a Reason

Criss Cross 1010 (CD)

Chet Baker (tp), Warne Marsh (ts), Hod O'Brien (p), Cecil McBee (b), Eddie Gladden (dr), 9/30/1984:
WELL SPOKEN / IF YOU COULD SEE ME NOW / WE KNOW IT'S LOVE (2x) / LOOKING GOOD TONIGHT (2x) / IMAGINATION / BLUES FOR A REASON

Chet Baker
Live at Buffalo

CCB Prod. CCB/CD 1223

Baker (tp, voc), Sal Nistico (ts), Lorne Lofsky (g), Chris Conners (b), Art Frank (d); 11/11/84:
STELLA BY STARLIGHT / I REMEMBER YOU / NIGHTBIRD / I'M OLD FASHIONED / MARGERINE

Åke Johansson trio with Chet Baker and Toots Thielemans
Chet & Toots

Dragon DRCD 333

Baker (tp, voc), Thielemans (harmonica), Johansson (p), Kjell Jansson (b), Rune Carlsson (d); 2/26/85:
BEATRICE / LAMENT / ALL THE THINGS YOU ARE / WHEN I FALL IN LOVE / BROKEN WING / FOR MINORS ONLY / MY FOOLISH HEART

After Chet's death, many mediocre concerts were put out on record. On the two CDs mentioned above, you will also hear performances with little or no preparation and long solos. But on these occasions Chet is in good lip and the other musicians know how to back him up. At the Buffalo concert, Art Frank—also heard on *Burnin' at*

Backstreet—is behind the drum set and doing a fine job. Thielemans—a subtle, melodic improviser—also makes a sympathetic accompanist.

Chet Baker / Paul Bley
Diane

Steeplechase 31207

Chet Baker (tp, voc), Paul Bley (p); 3/27/1985:

IF I SHOULD LOSE YOU / YOU GO TO MY HEAD / HOW DEEP IS THE OCEAN / PENT UP HOUSE / EVERYTIME WE SAY GOODBYE / DIANE / SKIDDLIN' / LITTLE GIRL BLUE

A quiet high point. This plate consists almost exclusively of ballads. Even "If I Should Lose You"—usually played up-tempo by Chet—is taken extremely slowly. The trumpet sound is at the limits of audibility, the piano chords sound melancholy. Bley reveals himself as an almost ideal partner for Chet. The British jazz magazine *Wire*: "There's almost no motion in the music; their meditations are on the edge of the drop into complete silence." On account of the success of this record this duo were invited a year later to Toronto. On that occasion the trumpeter fell asleep on the stage and had to be carried off.

Chet Baker
Chet's Choice

Criss Cross 1016

Chet Baker (tp); Philip Catherine (g), Hein van de Geyn (b); 6/6/85:

ADRIANO / BLUES IN THE CLOSET / STELLA BY STARLIGHT

personnel as above, but Jean-Louis Rassinfosse (b) replaces van de Geyn; 6/25/85:

IF I SHOULD LOSE YOU / SAD WALK / HOW DEEP IS THE OCEAN / DOODLIN' / MY FOOLISH HEART / CONCEPTION / LOVE FOR SALE

This is the best recording of the Baker/Catherine/ Rassinfosse trio. Chet has particular success with the fast numbers from the June 25 session. A comparison with the trio with Doug Raney and Ørsted-Pedersen is inevitable, and shows remarkable differences: Rassinfosse is no virtuoso and limits himself to functional accompaniment. Raney is a conservative bebopper; Catherine, in contrast, hardly cares about stylistic borders: he plays funk licks, country & western phrases, Django Reinhardt passages, and makes indiscriminate use of electronics. In short: Catherine and Rassinfosse furnish an unpretentious, playful accompaniment.

Chet Baker
Candy
Sonet SNTCD 946

Chet Baker (tp, voc) Michel Graillier (p), Jean-Louis Rassinfosse (b), 6/30/1985:
LOVE FOR SALE / NARDIS / CANDY / BYE BYE BLACKBIRD / SAD WALK / TEMPUS FUGIT / RED'S BLUES

Amstel Octet / Chet Baker
Hazy Hugs
Challenge Records CHR 70058

Chet Baker, Edu Ninck Blok (tp), Evert Hekkema (bs), Kees van Lier (as), Dick de Graaf (ts), Jan Vennik (bs), Bert van den Brink (p); Hein van de Geyn (b), John Engels (b); 9/22/1985:
SILVER BLUES / SOMEDAY YOU'LL LEAVE Me (2x) / DEEP SOUL (2x) / SHIFTING DOWN (2x) / TERGIVERSATION (2x) / HAZY HUGS

Chet Baker
Live from the Moonlight

Philology 214 W 10/11

Chet Baker (tp, voc), Michel Graillier (p), Massimo Moriconi (b);
11/24/85:
POLKA DOT AND MOONBEAMS (2x) / NIGHT BIRD / ESTATE / DEE'S
DILEMMA / HOW DEEP IS THE OCEAN / MY FOOLISH HEART / MY
FUNNY VALENTINE / ARBOR WAY / BROKEN WING / FUNK IN DEEP
FREEZE

Note: two CDs in one box

A concert in which Chet plays every note with total concentration. The accompaniment whispers; the tempo is
barely perceptible, and Chet achieves the greatest thing
possible in music: there is no barrier anymore between
his instrument and his emotions.

Chet Baker
As Time Goes By

Timeless CD SJP 251/252

Chet Baker (tp, voc), Harold Danko (p), John Burr (b), Ben Riley (dr);
12/17, 18/1986:
YOU AND THE NIGHT AND THE MUSIC / AS TIME GOES BY / MY
MELANCHOLY BABY / I'M A FOOL TO WANT YOU / WHEN SHE SMILES
/ SEA BREEZE / YOU HAVE BEEN HERE ALL ALONG / ANGEL EYES /
YOU'D BE SO NICE TO COME HOME TO / ROUND MIDNIGHT

Chet Baker
Live in Tokyo

Evidence ECD 22158-2

Chet Baker (tp, voc) Harold Danko (p), Hein van de Geyn (b), John
Engels (dr); 6/14/1987:

STELLA BY STARLIGHT / FOR MINORS ONLY / ALMOST BLUE / PORTRAIT IN BLACK & WHITE / MY FUNNY VALENTINE / FOUR / ARBORWAY / I'M A FOOL TO WANT YOU / SEVEN STEPS TO HEAVEN / FOR ALL WE KNOW / BROKEN WING

As in a good solo, the climax in this survey comes shortly before the end. *Live in Tokyo,* a double CD (a combination of the records previously issued separately as *Memories* and *Four*) may be the best record Chet ever made. He plays here with a synthesis of the strength of his early years and the depth of his late. Thanks to Peter Huijts, methadone, and a congenial rhythm section, he is in top form. It is strange that the only piece that doesn't quite work opens the record. But that is a minor drawback. The trumpet solo on "My Funny Valentine" is a précis of all the qualities Chet had refined over a forty-year career.

Chet Baker
The Legacy, Vol. 1
Baker (tp) with the NDR Big Band, personnel as on the next recording; 11/14/87:
HERE'S THAT RAINY DAY / HOW DEEP IS THE OCEAN / MISTER B. / IN YOUR OWN SWEET WAY / ALL OF YOU / DOLPHIN DANCE / LOOK FOR THE SILVER LINING / DJANGO / ALL BLUES

Note: on the jacket, Chet is pictured with members of the Concord All Stars: Al Cohn, Scott Hamilton, and Buddy Tate. Of course, they don't play on the record.

Chet Baker
The Last Concert

Enja ENJ 6074-22

Chet Baker (tp, voc), with the Hanover Radio Orchestra and the big band of the North German Radio under the direction of Dieter Glawischnig with (among others) Herb Geller (as), John Schröder (g), Walter Norris (p), Lucas Lindholm (b) and Aage Tanggaard (dr); 4/28/1988:
ALL BLUES / MY FUNNY VALENTINE / WELL YOU NEEDN'T / SUMMER-TIME / IN YOUR OWN SWEET WAY / DJANGO / I FALL IN LOVE TOO EASILY / LOOK FOR THE SILVER LINING / I GET ALONG WITHOUT YOU VERY WELL / CONCEPTION / THERE'S A SMALL HOTEL / SIPPIN' AT BELLS / TENDERLY

Chet Baker (tp), Walter Norris (p), Lucas Lindholm (b), Aage Tanggaard (dr), 11/14/1987:
MY FUNNY VALENTINE

Note: This double CD is a combination of the records previously issued separately as *Straight from the Heart* and *My Favourite Songs*. In spite of the title, this was not Chet's last performance. On no edition is it noted, meanwhile, that the last number derives from a different session.

These are Chet's last recordings, and another high point of his discography. The strings are sometimes too obtrusive, but everything else is as it should be. The arrangements are successful, the repertoire—chosen for the concert by the trumpeter himself—is appropriate, and the sound engineers earn top marks. In the relaxed trumpet solos one can hear that the monitors are correctly installed, and the sound on the CD is also ideal. One of the few other soloists is Herb Geller, an old associate from the West Coast. Every one of Chet's solos is a masterpiece, and with "I Fall in Love Too Easily"—incidentally the first piece he had recorded as a singer—he creates for himself a fitting requiem.

After the concert in Hanover, Chet played again in Calais (April 30), at the New Morning in Paris (May 5), the Thelonious in Rotterdam (May 7), and finally on the night of the 10th to the 11th of May he jammed on two pieces with the group Bad Circuits in the Dizzy, also in Rotterdam. Of these last four appearances no recordings, as far as I know, were made, and considering his condition in those last days, it is perhaps as well.

This, instead, is a worthy conclusion to Chet's recording career.

chet baker's complete
works: an overview

*T*he previous chapter was devoted to Baker's essential releases. In this chapter I give a short overview of his complete recorded oeuvre, for the benefit of collectors especially. It is important to know what to buy and, just as importantly, what not to. Each CD (LP, vinyl single, or EP) is given a rating, varying from one star—which means an absolute disgrace—to five stars, reserved for masterpieces. Double CDs, triple CDs and boxed sets are counted and reviewed as a single item. In case of recordings that were published under different names and labels, I try to cite the most recent issue.

★★½ **1. Live at the Trade Winds (Fresh Sound) 1952**
Jam sessions, including "Out of Nowhere," Chet's earliest recording. A part of this CD was also available as *Al Haig Live in Hollywood* (Xanadu).

★★★ **2. Bird and Chet live at the Trade Winds (with Charlie Parker, Fresh Sound) 1952**
See previous chapter.

★★★★½ **3. The Complete Pacific Jazz Recordings of the Gerry Mulligan Quartet with Chet Baker (Pacific) 1952–1957**

See previous chapter. Mosaic has also issued a boxed set of this quartet.

★★★★ **4. Gerry Mulligan/Paul Desmond (Fantasy) 1952–1953**
Features the nine essential titles the Mulligan/Baker quartet (without Desmond, of course) did for Fantasy. Four of them can also be found on *Mulligan/Baker* (Prestige).

★★★★ **5. Konitz meets Mulligan (Pacific) 1953**
Lee Konitz sits in with Mulligan's quartet and seems to feel at home there.

★★★ **6. L.A. Get-Together (with Stan Getz, Fresh Sound) 1953**
Getz does a fine job subbing for Gerry Mulligan in the quartet, live at The Haig.

★★★½ **7. Chet Baker & Strings (Columbia) 1953**
Somewhat pretentious strings with Chet—in his James Dean-days—playing the melody. A part of this is also available as *Grey December* (Pacific).

★★★★ **8. The Best of Chet Baker Plays (Pacific) 1953**
Good selection of instrumental tracks with Russ Freeman.

★★½ **9. Chet Baker and the Lighthouse All Stars: Witch Doctor (Contemporary) 1953**
Jam session, a little ragged, with West Coast colleagues.

★★½ **10. Miles Davis and the Lighthouse All Stars: At Last (Contemporary) 1953**

More music from a lengthy jam session, with Chet only on the title track.

★★★ **11. Charlie Parker: The Bird You Never Heard (Stash) 1953**

Collection of very rare Parker recordings. Chet in three tracks, but the tape fades down as soon as Chet starts his solo. Was also available as *Birth of the Bebop* (Stash).

★★½ **12. The Newport Years, Vol. 1 (Philology) 1953–1956**

Various live recordings (with bootleg sound) in Europe and the USA.

★★★★ **13. Ensemble and Sextet (Fresh Sound) 1953–1956**

Nice studio tracks with typical, neat West Coast arrangements. A part of this was also available as *Grey December* (Pacific).

★★★★★ **14. The Best of Chet Baker Sings (Pacific) 1953–1956**

The classic early vocal recordings in the studio with Russ Freeman. Essential for readers of this book. A part of this was available as *Chet Baker Sings* (Pacific). Some vocal tracks were issued—as *Pretty/Groovy*, on Pacific—with Bill Perkins (ts) and Jimmy Giuffre (cl) overdubbed in place of Chet's vocals. See also previous chapter.

★★★★★ **15. The Complete Pacific Jazz Studio Chet Baker/Russ Freeman (Mosaic) 1953–1956**

See previous chapter.

★★★ **16. Newport years, Vol. 1 (Philology) 1953–1956**
Various live recordings in the USA and Europe. Bootleg sound, but charming meetings with Caterina Valente, Dave Brubeck, and the Kurt Edelhagen Orchestra.

★★★ **17. Boston, 1954 (Uptown) 1954**
Series of unspectacular airshots of the quartet with Russ Freeman.

★★★★ **18. Jazz at Ann Arbor (Pacific) 1954**
Same band, better playing, professional sound.

★★★★ **19. The Complete Pacific Jazz Live Chet Baker/Russ Freeman (Mosaic) 1954**
See previous chapter.

★★★★ **20. Sings and Plays (Pacific) 1954–1955**
More singing in the studio with strings only on four tracks.

★★★ **21. Big Band (Pacific) 1954–1956**
Tight big-band orchestrations, allowing Chet some solo spots.

★★½ **22. Trumpet Geniuses of the Fifties (with Clifford Brown, Philology) 1954–1956**
TV performances with small groups, with a practice tape of Brownie as a bonus. Completists only.

★★★ **23. In Europe, 1955 (Philology) 1955**
Parts from two concerts. Strong trumpet solos, but

recording quality varies from fair to terrible. Most side-men are fine.

★★★ **24. Lars Gullin: The Great Lars Gullin (Dragon) 1955**
Includes four tracks with the Scandinavian baritonist sitting in with Chet's quartet, live in Germany.

★★★½ **25–28. In Paris, Vols. 1, 2, 3, 4 (EmArcy) 1955–1956**
Four CDs with studio work, mostly with French sidemen who do a good job in the then-fashionable cool style.

★★★½ **29–30. Live in Europe 1956, Vol 1 & 2 (Jazz Anthology/ Jazz View) 1956**
Italian concert with solid European professionals. Sound is respectable.

★★★ **31. Cools Out (Pacific) 1956**

★★★½ **32. Chet Baker & Crew (Pacific) 1956**

★★★ **33. At the Forum Theatre (Fresh Sound) 1956**
The boppish quintet with Phil Urso in good spirits. The Forum Theatre CD has only half as much music as *CB & Crew*.

★★★ **34. The Route (Pacific) 1956**
Chet, Art Pepper, and Richie Kamuca in the studio. Not bad, but not as lively as it might have been.

★★★★½ **35. Quartet (Pacific) 1956**
One last great meeting with Freeman, led by the piano player. See also previous chapter.

★★½ **36. Theme Music from 'The James Dean Story' (Pacific) 1956**

Chet and Bud Shank are soloists in this soundtrack by Johnny Mandel. Not very exciting without the movie.

★★★★ **37. Playboys (with Art Pepper, Pacific) 1956**

Fine bebop date with lots of fire, and charts by Jimmy Heath.

★★★ **38. Jack Sheldon: Jack's Groove (GNP) 1957**

Small big band featuring Sheldon, a trumpet colleague from the West Coast. Chet plays along in four tracks and gets some solo spots. Was also available as *Jack Sheldon and His All Star Band* (Crescendo/Gene Norman Presents)

★★★ **39. Gerry Mulligan Quartet: Reunion (Pacific/Manhattan) 1957**

Reunion with solid playing but lacking the old magic.

★★★ **40. Annie Ross: Sings a Song with Mulligan (Pacific/Manhattan) 1957**

Studio date with Ross doing no harm while Chet and Mulligan are having another reunion.

★★½ **41. Embraceable You (Pacific) 1957**

Forgotten vocal studio date that goes on and on, although the musicians seem to be exhausted. Has its moments, though.

★★ **42. Stan meets Chet (with Stan Getz, Verve) 1958**

Both horn men sound amazingly uninspired during this sloppy studio date.

★★★ **43–44. Chet Plays the Best of Lerner and Loewe (Riverside/OJC) 1958**

Chet's lips are okay but he sounds uninvolved in this collection of evergreens.

★★★★ **45. In New York (Riverside/OJC) 1958**

Sparkling collaboration with East Coasters like Johnny Griffin, Paul Chambers, and Philly Joe Jones.

★★★★ **46. Sings It Could Happen to You (Riverside/OJC) 1958**

Chet's voice is not very youthful anymore, but some of these renditions—"Old Devil Moon," for example— became classics.

★★★ **47. Chet Baker Introduces Johnny Pace (Riverside/OJC) 1958**

Young, Sinatra-like singer backed by Chet and a studio band.

★★★½ **48. Chet in Milan (OJC) 1959**

Fine studio dates with devoted Italian sidemen.

★★ **49. With Fifty Italian Strings (Jazzland/OJC) 1959**

Too many saccharine strings drown out Chet's playing and singing. Was also available as *Angel Eyes* (DJM Limited)

★★★ **50. Live in Paris, 1960–63, Live in Nice, 1975 (Esoldun-Ina) 1960–1975**

Various radio recordings, ranging from compelling to chaotic.

★★★ **51. Italian Movies (Liuto records) 1960–1962**
Chet as soloist in soundtracks by Piero Umiliani.
Playing is fair, sound so-so.

★★★ **52. With Ennio Morricone and His Orchestra (RCA) 1962**
Chet sings—in Italian!—and plays four songs he apparently wrote in jail. Only on vinyl EP. Extremely rare.

★★★★½ **53. Chet is Back (RCA) 1962**
See previous chapter. Also available as *The Italian Sessions* (RCA) and *Somewhere Over the Rainbow* (RCA/Bluebird).

★★★ **54. Stella by Starlight (Westwind) 1962[?]**
Radio gig with Jacques Pelzer. The notes gives the wrong personnel and say: '1964, Rome'. The session took place in Belgium, probably 1962. Stuffy sound.

★★★ **55. Trumpet Anthology (Westwind) 1962[?]**
Includes three alternate takes from the previous session.

★★★ **56. Dizionario Enciclopedico del Jazz (DEJ-08) 1963**
Features Chet on three tracks, playing bop standards with an Italian/French group.

57. Brussels 1964 (Landscape) 1963[?]
★★★½ Nice radio recordings with Jacques Pelzer in Belgium. The year given in the title is definitely incorrect.

★★★ **58. Plays and Sings (Jazz Junction/Colpix) 1964**

★★★½ **59. Baby Breeze (Verve) 1964**

Studio sessions, back in the States. Chet sometimes seems to be struggling with the flugelhorn on *Plays and Sings*. *Baby Breeze*—which contains both mellow vocals and bebop material—is also available as *Compact Jazz* (EmArcy).

★★★★ **60. Baker's Holiday (EmArcy/Polygram) 1965**

Chet plays Billie Holiday—a good match. See previous chapter.

★★★ **61–63. On a Misty Night, Lonely Star, Stairway to the Stars (Prestige) 1965**

Three CDs with all the tracks from the sessions with George Coleman. Good, boppish playing from all the sidemen. Chet sounds a bit tired. Also available on five CDs (on Prestige) under the original titles: *Groovin'*, *Comin' On*, *Smokin'*, *Cool Burnin'*, and *Boppin'*.

★ **64. Joe Pass: A Sign of the Times (World Pacific) 1965**

Dead, commercial stuff, performed on automatic pilot.

★ **65–68. The Mariachi Brass: A Taste of Tequila (also available as: The Modern Sound of Mexico); Hats Off; Double Shot; In the Mood (World Pacific) 1965–1966**

Horrible. Chet trying to make some money—and some music, despite everything—backed by Herb Alpert-style horns. Avoid at all costs. Never made it into the CD era.

★ **69–71. Bud Shank Featuring Chet Baker: Michelle; California Dreamin'; Magical Mystery (World Pacific) 1965–1967**

These were hard times for Shank too. But he didn't seem too concerned—'We all have to pay the rent'— whereas Chet suffers with every note on these bread-and-butter gigs.

★ **72–73. Bud Shank: Is Paris Burnin'?; Brazil, Brazil, Brazil (1966)**
The former is a vinyl single, the latter an LP with Chet only on one track. More of the same.

★ **74–75. The Carmel Strings: Quietly There; Into My Life (World Pacific) 1966**
Like the Mariachi material, but instead of horns imagine some equally stupid strings.

★★★★ **76. Live at Pueblo, Colorado (CC Baker) 1966**
Real music. Sound is so-so, but Chet and his band are surprisingly forceful. A pity he hardly ever got a chance to play like this in studio sessions during the '60s. See also previous chapter.

★ **77. Albert's House (Bainbridge/Repertoire) 1968 or 1969**
Chet's worst record. His chops are at an all-time low (as are his spirits), and he tries to play some silly songs (by Steve Allen) backed by a dreadful organ. Amazingly, this record was issued again and again, even on CD. The other commercial records can only be found in secondhand stores with lots of vinyl.

★ **78. Blood, Chet and Tears (Verve) 1970[?]**
Highly professional garbage.

★★★ **79. Konitz, Baker, Jarrett Quintet (Jazz Connoisseur) 1974**

Unrehearsed meeting of the giants. Airshots, with one track of Konitz and Bill Evans as a bonus.

★★★½ **80. In Concert (with Lee Konitz, India Navigation) 1974**

One more unrehearsed concert. This one gets better and better in the course of the performance.

★★★★ **81. Carnegie Hall Concert (Epic) 1974**

Reunion with Gerry Mulligan on a grand stage, domi-nated by the baritonist. Was previously issued as two separate records and as a double LP: *Carnegie Hall Concert Vol. 1 & 2* (CTI).

★★★★½ **82. She Was Too Good To Me (CTI/Epic) 1974**

Excellent comeback record on the deluxe CTI label. See also previous chapter.

★★★★ **83. Together (with Paul Desmond, Epic) 1974–1977**

A compilation of two great 'cool' artists performing together in the studio.

★★★½ **84. Jim Hall: Concierto (CTI/Epic) 1975**

Jim Hall is inspired and Chet too, much of the time. Weird '70s studio sound, unfortunately.

★★½ **85. It Happened in Pescara, Italy (Philology) 1975**

Chet only on one number, "Milestones," with Kenny Drew, live.

★★½   **86. The Fabulous Pescara Jam Sessions (Philology) 1975**
More live stuff from this Italian city, with Chet on three edited tracks.

★★★   **87. Chet Baker in Italy/Unissued 1975–1988 (Philology)**
Various live registrations of varying sound and quality.

★★★   **88. My Funny Valentine (Philology) 1975–1987**
More Philology material, this time with seven very different versions of Chet's signature song.

★★★½   **89. Deep In A Dream Of You (Moon Records) 1976**
Gig in Rome with Pelzer. Chet's playing is sometimes very touching, the sound could be worse.

★★★   **90. Steve Houben: S.H. (Sabam) 1977**
Studio date with Belgian alto player and Chet on only one song, "I Haven't."

★★★★½   **91. You Can't Go Home Again (A&M) 1977**
Chet doing surprisingly well in a jazz-rock setting with Michael Brecker.

★★★½   **92. The Best Thing For You (A & M Jazz) 1977**
Five inspired, rather short songs in an American studio and one—"El Morro"—that is much too long.

★★★   **93. Plays and sings (Carosello) 1977**
Nice Italian studio tracks with Jacques Pelzer and Ruth Young.

★★★★ **94. Once Upon a Summertime (ArtistHouse/OJC) 1977**
Powerful, Miles-influenced studio date in the US. See previous chapter.

★★★½ **95. The Rising Sun Collection (Just a Memory) 1978**
Live and in good spirits with baritonist Roger Rogenberg in a Canadian club.

★★★ **96. Astrud Gilberto: That Girl from Ipanema (Image/Rare Bird) 1978[?]**
The bossanova queen, with Baker guesting on "Far Away."

★★½ **97. Live in Chateauvallon (Esoldun-Ina) 1978**

★★★ **98. Live at Nick's (Criss Cross) 1978**
Radio recordings. Fine band, but the solos by the sidemen are too long. This group (with Phil Markowitz) can be heard better on the following record.

★★★★★ **99. Broken Wing (Cornelia/Westwind/Inner city) 1978**
See previous chapter. Was also available as: *In Paris, Vol. 2* (Westwind)

★★★ **100. Two a Day (Dreyfus) 1978**
A fair studio session with Phil Markowitz.

★★★★½ **101–103. This Is Always; Someday My Prince Will Come; Daybreak (Steeplechase) 1979**
Three great CDs, all recorded during one (!) concert in Copenhagen with Doug Raney and Niels-Henning Ørsted Pedersen. A truly Olympic accomplishment. See also previous chapter.

★★★★ **104. The Touch of Your Lips (Steeplechase) 1979**
The same band, the same mood, now in the studio.

★★★½ **105. Round Midnight (Challenge) 1979**
Mediocre playing from most of the guys, but Chet sounds OK. Vocals by Rachel Gould. The complete session (in a London studio) was also available on two records: *All Blues* and *Rendez-vous* (Bingow)

★★★★½ **106. No Problem (Steeplechase) 1979**
Wonderful renditions in a Copenhagen studio of Duke Jordan compositions.

★★★ **107. Tender Variations (Decca) 1979**
Soundtrack for the film *Flic ou Voyou*. Much action with Jean-Paul Belmondo and music by Philippe Sarde. Not bad of its kind.

★★★ **108. Lackerschmid/Baker (Sandra/Inak) 1979**

★★★½ **109. Ballads for Two (with Wolfgang Lackerschmid, Sandra/Inak) 1979**
Nice sessions with young vibraphonist Wolfgang Lackerschmid. A better buy is the next one, though.

★★★★ **110. Why Shouldn't You Cry (Enja) 1979/1987**
A "Best Of" from the collaboration with Lackerschmid, including some intimate 'free' blowing. See also previous chapter.

★½ **111. Just Friends (Arco) 1979**
Live. Chet in bad shape with a band that doesn't know what to do about it.

★★ **112. CB & Boto Brazilian Quartet (Dreyfus) 1980**
Somewhat glib Latin date with composer Rique
Pantoja. Was also available as *Salsamba*.

★★★ **113. Soft Journey (Ida) 1980**
Subtle, rather tired-sounding studio date led by Enrico
Pieranunzi, featuring his music.

★★★★★ **114. Leaving (Intercord) 1980**
The best Chet Baker record you never heard. Good
band, good studio sound, intense soloing. Never issued
on CD! See also previous chapter.

★★★½ **115. Ron Carter: Patrao (Milestone) 1980**
Chet doing fine in some Latin-tinged songs by bassist
Ron Carter.

★★★★ **116. Burnin' at Backstreet (Fresh Sound) 1980**
Incredible, powerful concert in New Haven with Art
Frank. For one of the few moments in his life, Chet
sounds aggressive and even seems to overpower the
other guys. See also previous chapter.

★★★ **117. Baker/Houben (Carrere/RECD) 1980**
Pleasant meeting with Belgian alto player Steve
Houben, with young Bill Frisell on guitar.

★★ **118–125. Down; I Remember You; My Funny Valentine;
Round Midnight; Just Friends; Tune Up; Conception; It
Never Entered My Mind (Circle Records) 1980–1981**
French and German concerts, issued on vinyl with an

apparently very low budget, to judge by the harsh sound and cheap sleeves. The tracks are very long; the producer simply put the tape recorder on. On *Just Friends*, you can hear Chet grumbling at someone.

★★½ 126. Night Bird (Westwind) 1980
Clumsy recorded concert in Paris with some good moments. A selection on CD of the series mentioned above.

★★★ 127. In Your Own Sweet Way (Circle Records) 1980
The best track of the Circle catalogue can be found on this one: Chet plays an inspired, fifteen-minute solo on "No Ties"—his longest on vinyl.

★★★ 128. Michel Graillier: Dream Drop (Owl) 1980
Chet sits in on the title song, Graillier's own composition.

★★½ 129. Live at Fat Tuesday's (Fresh Sound) 1981
Baker was exhausted, having arrived in the club immediately after a transatlantic flight. Fortunately, Bud Shank came by and sat in.

★★★½ 130. Chet Baker (Carlyne) 1981
Spirited meeting with solid French rhythm section.

★★★ 131. Out of Nowhere (Milestone) 1982
Chet sounds strong on this meeting with a semi-pro band from Oklahoma.

★★½ **132. Peace (Enja) 1982**

Meeting with American vibraphonist/composer David Friedman. Chet seems to prefer strong melodies to this intellectual stuff. Bass is too loud.

★★★½ **133. But Not for Me (Stash) 1982**

Fair studio date with good sidemen (Charlie Haden, Kenny Barron, and others), but Baker's playing lacks spark.

★★★ **134. Studio Trieste (with Jim Hall and Hubert Laws, CTI) 1982**

Spanish-tinged date with good musicians and charts by Don Sebesky. Not bad, although Sebesky did better work with Chet in 1977. On Jim Hall's record *Youkali* (CTI), parts from this record—and the next one with Roland Hanna—were used with different accompanists dubbed in.

★★★ **135. Roland Hanna: Gershwin, Carmichael, Cats (CTI) 1982**

Chet sits in on "Skylark," a tune he didn't know too well.

★★★★½ **136. Baker/Catherine/Rassinfosse (Igloo) 1983**

Chet sounding happy with this new, sympathetic trio. Some songs are given a samba beat.

★★★½ **137. Live in Sweden (Dragon) 1983**

In concert with fine pianist Åke Johansson. Solos by the sidemen are too long.

★★ **138. September Song (Marshmellow/Century) 1983**
Club date with Duke Jordan, who is rather monotonous.
Mediocre sound.

★★★ **139. Quintessence Vol. 1 (with Stan Getz, Concord) 1983**

★★★½ **140. Quintessence Vol. 2 (as above)**
A Scandinavian concert on two CDs. Good playing
from Getz and his trio—especially on the second
volume—but Chet sounds uninvolved.

★★★½ **141. The Stockholm Concerts (with Stan Getz, Verve)
1983**
A package with three CDs (with the same band as on
Quintessence), featuring Chet on half of the tracks. A
selection was previously issued on one CD: *Line for
Lyons* (Sonet). See also previous chapter.

★★★½ **142. Kirk Lightsey Trio: Everything Happens to Me
(Timeless) 1983**
Chet sits in on a crisp "Ray's Idea" and the long and
touching title track. Both tunes were later included on
some editions of *Mr B.*; the title track alone was added
to the CD version of *Sings Again* (Timeless).

★★ **143. Jim Porto: Rio (Siglo Quattro) 1983**
Hard-to-get stuff of a (probably Italian) singer with
Chet on two songs. Completists only.

★★★ **144. Star Eyes (Marshmellow/Century) 1983**
Live with Duke Jordan. Three long tunes with Chet trying hard to sound firm and boppish. Bass is not clearly
audible.

★★★ **145. Live at New Morning (Marshmellow/Century) 1983**
Another concert with Jordan. Good playing, but sound is unsatisfactory.

★½ **146–147. A Trumpet for the Sky, Vol. 1 & Vol. 2 (Philology) 1983**
Italian concert, recorded with a Walkman placed directly on the bass amp—that, at any rate, is the way these two CDs sound. Avoid.

★★★½ **148. Al Capolinea (Red Records) 1983**
Fair studio date in Italy with Diane Vavra sitting in on soprano sax.

★★★ **149. Elvis Costello: Punch the Clock (F-Beat) 1983**
Chet only on "Shipbuilding," to which he makes some lovely contributions. Costello later came by to help Chet during a problematic gig in Ronnie Scott's, and Chet added Costello's "Almost Blue" to his vocal repertoire. "Shipbuilding" can also be heard on Costello's *Girls, Girls, Girls* and *The Best of Elvis Costello* (both Columbia).

★★★½ **150. The Improvisor (Cadence) 1983**
Live in Sweden. Long, sparkling solos with fine local band. See also previous chapter.

★★★½ **151. Mr B. (Timeless) 1983–1985**
Delicate studio session with Michel Graillier; some tracks added later. Good sound. See also previous chapter.

★★½ **152. Naima (Philology) 1983–1987**
More live recordings from Philology. Completists only.

★★★ **153. Live at Buffalo (CC Baker) 1984**
Concert with Sal Nistico. Reasonable sound, good band, but too many overly long solos by the sidemen.

★★★ **154. Blues for a Reason (with Warne Marsh, Criss Cross) 1984**
Somewhat overrated studio date with the famous Lennie Tristano disciple. Chet did better things this year.

★★★ **155. Le Jumeau (with Vladimir Cosma, Carrere) 1984**
Chet doing another soundtrack with composer Cosma. Some good moments, support by Niels-Henning Ørsted Pedersen.

★★★ **156. Plays Vladimir Cosma (Carrere) mid-70s[?]–1984**
Selections from Cosma's soundtracks with Baker, including some music off the previous record. Exact recording dates and personnel are not given on the sleeve.

★★½ **157. Rique Pantoja & Chet Baker (WEA Latin) 1984–1987**
More Latin music with Pantoja and a rather synthetic-sounding band. Chet liked his song "Arbor Way," though.

★★ **158. Lizzy Mercier Descloux: One for the Soul (Polydor) 1985**
Superficial pop singing with only a few glimpses of Baker.

★★★ **159. Jean-Jacques Goldman: Non Homologué (Epic) 1985**
Another popular singer, with Chet sitting in on one *chanson*.

★★ **160. There'll Never Be Another You (Timeless) 1985**
Chet and Philip Catherine during a concert in Zagreb, feeling awkward because the bass player didn't show up.

★★½ **161–163. My Foolish Heart; Time After Time; Misty (IRD Records) 1985**
Every note of a Dallas club gig (and a few studio items from the following day thrown in) with a workmanlike band on three CDs. A selection on one record would have been enough.

★½ **164. Fred Raulston Quartet: Would You Believe? (Jazz Mark) 1985**
The same band, mostly in the studio. Chet was in very bad shape.

★★★ **165. In Bologna (Dreyfus) 1985**
In concert with Philip Catherine and Jean-Louis Rassinfosse. Inspired, but (as often) the solos could have been more concise.

★★★ **166. I Remember You (Enja) 1985**
Live. The playing is OK, but the sound is below Enja's usual standard.

★★★★ **167. Chet & Toots (with Toots Thielemans, Dragon) 1985**
Live. Sympathetic interplay with Thielemans, good sound.

★★½ **168. Sings Again (Timeless) 1985**

Excellent Max Bolleman sound, but Chet sings too much and his voice is not in good shape.

★★★★★ **169. Diane (with Paul Bley, Steeplechase) 1985**

Duo with pianist Bley in a Danish studio. Incredible series of ballads of two kindred spirits. See also previous chapter.

★★★★½ **170. Live from the Moonlight (Philology) 1985**

Double CD, live. Long, flawless trumpet solos in an Italian club, as good as the night in 1979 that yielded three Steeplechase records.

★★★★★ **171. Chet's Choice (Criss Cross) 1985**

Excellent playing and sound. The best collaboration with Catherine on record.

★★★ **172. Strollin' (Enja) 1985**

The same trio, with Catherine working hard and Chet sounding less energetic.

★★★½ **173. Hazy Hugs (Challenge) 1985**

With the Amstel octet, including Evert Hekkema on baritone horn. Chet played the compositions for the first time (and by ear) but does a good job.

★★ **174. Titziana Ghiglioni/Mike Melillo: Goodbye, Chet (Philology) 1985**

Duet album with singer Ghiglioni and pianist Melillo, and three rehearsal tracks with Chet added.

★★★★ **175. Candy (Sonet) 1985**
Intimate studio date with Michel Graillier and the usual repertoire in Scandinavia. Also on videotape with, as a bonus, a conversation with bass player Red Mitchell and a rendition of "My Romance" with Mitchell at the piano.

★★½ **176. Jazz Studio Orchestra: Ten Years Jazz Studio Orchestra (Pan-Am) 1985**
Extremely rare recordings with an Italian big band that has a tendency to overpower our subject, who appears on three tracks.

★★★ **177. Herbie Hancock et al.: Round Midnight (CBS) 1985**
Soundtrack of the film with the same name, featuring Dexter Gordon. Chet sings and plays on "Fair Weather."

★★★ **178. Symphonically (with Mike Melillo, Soul Note) 1985**
Meeting with a rather stiff Italian symphony orchestra and charts by Melillo.

★★ **179. Joe Locascio: Sleepless (Pausa) 1985 or 1986**
Chet makes some human noises in a computer jungle. Locascio wrote the tunes and plays keyboards. Some of it sounds like yoga music.

★★ **180. Heartbreak (Timeless) 1985–1986**
Vocal recordings for Timeless, reissued with strings added after Chet's death. Better to buy the original CDs.

★½ **181. When Sunny Gets Blue (Steeplechase) 1986**
Chet should have stayed in bed but came to the studio nevertheless. Only the title track should have been committed to record.

★★½ **182. Silent Nights (GSR CD) 1986**

With mediocre alto player Christopher Mason in a New Orleans studio, playing Christmas songs and some gospels. Chet managed to sound good, whatever he played.

★★★★ **183. As Time Goes By (Timeless) 1986**

★★★ **184. Cool Cat (Timeless) 1986**

Two CDs with some heartfelt singing (the best of his later years), and a trio with Harold Danko. Bolleman-sound. Also released as *Singing in the Midnight* (Polydor) and *Love Song* (Baystate).

★★ **185. Live at Ronnie Scott's (Hendring Wadham) 1986**

Enormously overrated gig with Chet almost falling asleep in the famous London jazz club. Also available on video (unfortunately). But he got some help. Van Morrison came by to sing a ballad, Elvis Costello (only on video) did a medley.

★★ **186. A Night at the Shalimar (Philology) 1987**

Live in Italy. Chet was sick and should have stayed in bed.

★★½ **187. Originals (Art & Sound) 1987**

Songs by Wolfgang Lackerschmid, played with little energy. Some touching moments, though. Also available as *Welcome Back* (Westwind). The highlights can be found on the compilation *Why Shouldn't You Cry* (Enja).

★★ **188. Let's Get Lost (RCA/Novus) 1987**

The movie soundtrack. Chet whispers and mumbles his way through too much unfamiliar material. Dull sound.

★★★★½ **189. The Legacy, Vol. 1 (Enja) 1987**

Chet with the NDR big band—as on his last recording —but without strings and almost as good.

★★½ **190. Felice Reggio: I Remember Chet (Philology) 1987–1991**

Tribute, recorded after Chet died, by an Italian trumpet player, with one track—from an Italian concert—with the man himself.

★★★★★ **191. Chet Baker in Tokyo (double CD, Evidence) 1987**

Chet in excellent shape, on a Japanese stage; his best recording ever. Listen to his trumpet solo in "My Funny Valentine." See also previous chapter. The concert was earlier available on two separate records: *Memories* (containing the best selection) and *Four*. A video of this concert circulates among fans (it was originally record- ed for Japanese TV).

★★ **192. Nino Buonocore: Una citta tra le mani (EMI) 1988**

Chet guests on three songs with this Italian(?) singer.

★★★ **193. Charlie Haden: Silence (Soul Note) 1987**

Nice session, although the meeting of Haden and Chet is underwhelming.

★★★ **194. In Memory Of (with Archie Shepp, L + R Records) 1988**

Live recordings with fair sound, good rhythm section, but too few good trumpet solos.

★★ **195. Chet on Poetry (Novus) 1988**

Italian studio gig with local poets. Too much talking and hardly any substantial music.

★★ **196. Blamann! Blamann! (with Jan Erik Vold, Hot Club) 1988**

Even more poetry. Only for people who understand Norwegian. When Chet plays, people should shut up and listen.

★★★ **197–199. Heart of a Ballad; Funk in Deep Freeze; Little Girl Blue (Philology) 1988**

Two duet records with great piano player Enrico Pieranunzi, and one with Pieranunzi's trio. Chet whispers on trumpet and vocals; alas, Max Bolleman wasn't there to capture it clearly.

★★ **200. Last Recording as Quartet (Timeless) 1988**

Clumsy recorded concert in Rosenheim, put on record after Chet's death. It should have stayed in the archives.

★★★★½ **201. The Last Great Concert (Enja) 1988**

Double CD. Lush arrangements with German big band and strings. Excellent sound, a fitting farewell. Was available on two separate CDs: *My Favourite Songs* (with the best selection) and *Straight from the Heart* (both Enja). See also previous chapter.

abbreviations

arr=arranger
as=alto saxophone
b=bass
bcl=bass clarinet
cga=conga
cond=conductor
cor=cornet
dr=drums
e-b=electric bass
e-g=electric guitar
e-org=electric organ
e-perc=electronic percussion
fl=flute
g=guitar
g-synth=guitar synthesizer
key=keyboards
ob=oboe
org=organ
p=piano
perc=percussion
sax=saxophone
ss=soprano saxophone
synth=synthesizer
tb=trombone
ts=tenor saxophone

tp=trumpet
v=violin
va=viola
vc=cello
vib=vibraphone
voc=vocals
xyl=xylophone

other cited sources

John S. Wilson, *The Collector's Jazz* (Philadelphia 1959)

"Gerry Mulligan: A Writer's Credo," *Down Beat* January 17, 1963

"Chet Baker's Tale of Woe," *Down Beat* July 30, 1964

Review of Chet Baker's Cork 'n' Bib engagement, *Down Beat*, May 21, 1964

Jazz Hot [Paris], November 1983, Chet Baker interview

The Wire [London], November 1985, Chet Baker interview

"Singing a Song of Mulligan," *Down Beat* January 1989

Hans Henrik Lerfeldt, *Chet: the discography of Chesney Henry Baker, compiled by Hans Henrik Lerfeldt and Thorbjørn Sjøgren* (Copenhagen 1985).

J. A. Deelder, *Modern passé* (Amsterdam 1984)

Let's Get Lost, A Film Journal by Bruce Weber (Little Bear Films 1988).

Chet Baker, *As though I had wings: the lost memoir* (New York 1997)

William Claxton, *Young Chet* (New York 1993; Munich 1998).

Harvey Bloomfield, http://www.chetbaker.net/. A comprehensive site devoted to Chet with photos, paintings, articles, and several discographies.

index of names